BRANDING EXPOSED

THE SECRET STRATEGIES THAT MAKE YOU SPEND

BY

LUCAS SHEFFIELD

Lucas Sheffield

Copyright 2024 Lucas Sheffield. All Rights reserved. No part of this publication may be reproduced without consent of the author.

"Design is the silent ambassador of your brand."

--Paul Rand

Table of Contents

Introduction

Chapter 1: The Evolution of Branding

Chapter 2: Psychological Foundations

Chapter 3: The Visual Language of Branding

Chapter 4: The Power of Names and Symbols

Chapter 5: The Power of Social Proof in Branding

Chapter 6: The Power of Scarcity and Urgency in Branding

Chapter 7: Humor and Authenticity

Chapter 8: The Power of Emotional Branding

Chapter 9: The Ethical Landscape of Branding

Chapter 10: Branding in Different Industries

Chapter 11: Cultural Influences on Branding

Chapter 12: The Future of Branding

Chapter 13: Case Studies in Successful Branding

Chapter 14: Empowering the Consumer

Conclusion

INTRODUCTION

In a world awash with logos, slogans, and carefully crafted images, branding has become an inescapable part of our daily lives. From the moment we wake up and reach for our favorite brand of coffee to the last scroll through our social media feeds before bed, we are constantly bombarded with brand messages. But have you ever stopped to consider just how profoundly these brands shape our thoughts, emotions, and behaviors?

Imagine walking into a store during the holiday season, your eyes immediately drawn to a sleek, white box adorned with a simple apple logo. Your heart rate quickens, and you feel a rush of excitement. You're not just looking at a piece of technology; you're looking at a symbol of innovation, status, and belonging. This is the power of branding at work.

Over the centuries, branding has evolved from simple ownership marks to complex symbols that carry immense cultural and personal significance. Today, brands don't just sell products; they sell identities, lifestyles, and even ideologies. They have the power to inspire loyalty, spark movements, and shape entire industries.

But with this power comes responsibility and the potential for manipulation. As consumers, we often find ourselves at the mercy of sophisticated marketing strategies that tap into our deepest desires and insecurities. The line between authentic connection and exploitation can be perilously thin.

This book aims to pull back the curtain on the world of branding, exploring its historical roots, psychological underpinnings, and societal impacts. We'll examine how visual elements and social influences shape our perceptions of brands, and grapple with the ethical implications of modern branding practices.

Our journey will take us through the corridors of history, the laboratories of psychology, and the boardrooms of major corporations. We'll hear from experts, analyze case studies, and reflect on our own experiences as consumers.

By the end of this book, you'll have a deeper understanding of how branding influences your behavior and a toolkit for navigating the brand-saturated world with greater awareness and discernment. You'll be empowered to make more informed decisions, not just as a consumer, but as an active participant in shaping the future of branding.

So, as we begin this exploration, I invite you to approach each chapter with an open mind and a critical eye. Reflect on your own experiences with brands and consider how they've shaped your perceptions and behaviors. Together, we'll unravel the complex tapestry of branding and discover what it truly means to be a conscious consumer in today's marketplace.

Chapter 1: The Evolution of Branding

From the sun-baked sands of ancient Egypt to the vibrant marketplaces we see today, the idea of branding has changed incredibly over the years. It has moved from simple identification to a major influence on how consumers make choices. To truly grasp what branding means today, we need to take a step back and look at its beginnings, where the foundations of this powerful marketing tool were first laid.

In ancient times, branding revolved around ownership. For instance, consider how people branded livestock thousands of years ago. As humans started to domesticate animals, there arose an urgent need to show ownership in a very visible way. A unique mark, often burned onto the skin of cows or sheep, served not just as a way to identify them but also as a sign of the owner's status and skill. In societies where livestock represented wealth, that mark became a source of pride and a reflection of one's social standing.

As trade routes expanded and markets thrived, the role of branding began to evolve further. Merchants, eager to stand out from their competitors, started using symbols and marks to build trust with their customers. Picture a lively market in ancient Greece, where vendors shouted about their goods amidst the noise of bargaining and chatter. A potter might carve a special design onto his pottery, not just to showcase his skills but also to signal his reputation in the community. This early form of branding assured customers that the product met certain standards, helping them make informed choices in a sea of options.

Looking back, we see that the roots of branding are deeply tied to our basic human desires for recognition and trust. The symbols and marks that emerged acted like a language of their own, sharing messages about quality, reliability, and authenticity. These early examples helped shape what would later become a sophisticated relationship between how consumers perceive a brand and the identity that company projects.

When the Industrial Revolution hit in the 18th century, branding underwent a dramatic transformation. Mass production changed the game, altering both how goods were made and how they were consumed. Products were no longer handcrafted by skilled artisans in small shops; instead, factories began pumping out items at an astonishing rate. This flood of similar products created an urgent need for differentiation, marking the birth of modern branding as we know it.

Manufacturers quickly realized that a strong brand could be their greatest asset in a crowded marketplace. Companies like Coca-Cola and Nestlé didn't just sell beverages and food; they became pioneers in the branding world. Coca-Cola recognized that its success wasn't just about the quality of its drink; it was about forming emotional connections with its drinkers. Through vivid imagery, catchy taglines, and a consistent brand presence, Coca-Cola fostered a sense of belonging and nostalgia that resonated globally.

Nestlé also understood the power of branding to carve out its space in the market. It was one of the first to see packaging as a branding tool, using eye-catching designs and colors to stand out on store shelves. Its commitment to quality and innovation helped solidify its reputation as a household name, showing that smart branding can create a bridge between consumers and products.

As the 20th century unfolded, the emotional side of branding took center stage. It was no longer enough for brands to simply distinguish themselves by features or price; they needed to forge emotional connections with their audience. Brands started to create identities that told stories—stories that resonated on a personal level. This shift allowed companies to move beyond straightforward transactions and build lasting loyalty that went far beyond the point of sale.

Imagine the impact of a television commercial that doesn't just promote a product but tells a story that pulls at the heartstrings. Storytelling in advertising became a hallmark of effective branding, inviting consumers into a narrative where they could see themselves as part of the brand's journey. Advertisers realized that people weren't just buying products; they were investing in lifestyles, values, and dreams. This psychological shift fundamentally changed how companies approached their marketing strategies.

Leading this evolution were brands that understood the importance of a unified identity. A brand's visual elements—like its logo, colors, and typography—began to shape how consumers perceived it. Think of iconic brands like Apple. Their minimalist design not only reflects a dedication to innovation but also conveys a sense of sophistication and exclusivity. The carefully crafted visual language can evoke strong emotional responses, creating a connection that's tough to break.

As time went on, new advertising platforms—like television, radio, and later, the internet—opened exciting new doors for brands to connect with their audiences. Each medium offered unique chances to tell stories, build communities, and nurture brand loyalty. Advertising experts learned to tap into the specifics of each platform, crafting messages that resonated with different audience groups and reflected contemporary culture.

Now, consider the explosion of social media in the 21st century. Platforms like Facebook and Instagram have transformed how brands engage with consumers, allowing for a two-way conversation that was once unimaginable. Brands are no longer just entities that deliver messages; they are now part of an ongoing dialogue, reacting to consumer feedback and adjusting their strategies in real-time. This shift has empowered consumers, giving them a voice that allows them to influence brand narratives and hold companies accountable.

The psychological factors involved in branding are intricate and layered. Research has shown that brands can stir emotions, and these feelings often guide consumer decisions. A study published in the "Journal of Consumer Research" found that people frequently base their choices not on cold hard facts but on the emotions tied to a brand. This insight emphasizes the significance of storytelling in branding; a powerful narrative can elevate a brand from just another item on a shelf to a vital part of someone's identity.

At this point in our exploration, it's essential to address the ethical considerations that come with branding. While branding has the potential to empower consumers by enabling informed choices, it can also be a tool for manipulation. Brands that play on psychological triggers without being transparent run the risk of losing consumer trust and harming their reputation. The real challenge lies in finding the right balance between effective branding and ethical responsibility.

As we reflect on the journey of branding, we uncover a rich narrative woven through history, culture, and psychology. From its beginnings as a simple way to mark ownership in ancient societies to its current role as a powerful influence on consumer behavior, branding has come a long way. This journey is marked by innovation and adaptation, revealing the complex relationship between brands and the people who engage with them.

Understanding this evolution is vital for consumers as they navigate today's marketplace. By recognizing the forces that shape branding, individuals can approach their purchasing decisions with a critical mindset. Knowing how brands create emotional connections and influence perceptions empowers consumers to make choices that truly reflect their values, separating real value from mere marketing fluff.

As we move forward in this chapter, we will dive deeper into the implications of this historical journey. We'll look at how branding continues to evolve in the digital age, the psychological factors that further shape consumer behavior, and the ethical dilemmas that arise in the quest for brand loyalty. Through these discussions, we aim to arm readers with the understanding they need to engage thoughtfully with branding, fostering a marketplace that prioritizes transparency, innovation, and consumer empowerment. Cultural movements and shifts in society have always played a crucial role in shaping branding strategies. Brands strive to connect with the values and beliefs of the communities they serve. To keep up with these changes, companies need to not only recognize how consumer feelings are evolving but also adjust their messaging to match. In this section, we'll take a closer look at how various cultural movements, like the feminist movement and the growing awareness of environmental issues, have influenced branding strategies and how consumers perceive brands. We'll share stories of brands that have successfully aligned their marketing with societal values, showing just how vital cultural awareness is for effective branding.

The feminist movement, which has gained significant traction in recent decades, has profoundly impacted branding. As society increasingly acknowledges the importance of gender equality, brands are beginning to understand that their messages must reflect a genuine commitment to these values. A perfect example is Dove, a brand that has been applauded for its focus on real beauty. Their "Real Beauty" campaign, launched in 2004, aimed to challenge conventional beauty standards that often left women feeling excluded. By showcasing women of different shapes, sizes, and ethnic backgrounds in their ads, Dove connected with a growing audience that craved authenticity and empowerment. This wasn't just a clever marketing tactic; it was a response to a cultural shift toward inclusivity and body positivity. Dove's success illustrates how brands can tap into cultural movements to create deeper connections with consumers.

On the flip side, brands that overlook these societal changes risk alienating their audience. A well-known soft drink brand found itself in hot water after releasing a controversial advertisement that many felt undermined social justice movements. The public's backlash was swift and severe, highlighting that consumers are increasingly aware of the messages brands send. This instance serves as a strong reminder of the need for brands to be culturally sensitive. In today's world, consumers expect brands to take a stand on pressing social issues.

The rise of environmental awareness has also reshaped branding strategies. As consumers become more mindful of their environmental footprint, brands are stepping up by adopting sustainable practices and promoting eco-friendly products. Take Patagonia, for example. This sportswear brand has positioned itself as a leader in environmental advocacy, famously urging customers to "buy less" and promoting the repair and reuse of their gear. This messaging not only aligns with consumer values but also sets Patagonia apart in a crowded market. The brand's commitment to sustainability has cultivated a loyal customer base that appreciates its authenticity and dedication to protecting the planet.

The success of brands like Patagonia underscores the importance of aligning branding strategies with cultural values. In a time when consumers are more informed and empowered than ever, brands need to do more than just offer quality products; they must embody the values that resonate with their audience. This adaptability is essential for staying relevant and building lasting relationships with consumers.

As we shift our focus to the digital age and globalization, it's important to recognize that these cultural changes are often amplified by the internet. The way consumers interact with brands has transformed dramatically, with social media platforms acting as both a megaphone for cultural movements and a stage for brands to showcase their values. For example, the hashtag #MeToo quickly gained traction online, prompting brands to rethink their internal practices and public messaging. Companies that embraced this moment and adjusted their policies accordingly received positive feedback from consumers, while those that stayed silent faced criticism and lost consumer trust.

The influence of social media on brand narratives is enormous. In this digital world, consumers have more tools than ever to express their opinions and hold brands accountable. This shift presents both challenges and opportunities for marketers. On one hand, brands must be vigilant and ready to respond to consumer feedback, as negative sentiments can spread like wildfire on social platforms. On the other hand, brands that engage genuinely with their audience can build strong communities, leading to greater loyalty.

Another important development in the branding landscape is the rise of influencer marketing, fueled by social media. Influencers, who often have significant sway over their followers, can shape opinions and drive buying decisions. Brands that partner with influencers who share their values can reach new audiences and build credibility. However, this relationship comes with its own set of challenges. Consumers are becoming more discerning, frequently demanding transparency and authenticity from both brands and influencers. Brands that overlook the importance of ethical partnerships risk backlash, as audiences are quick to call out anything that feels inauthentic.

Globalization adds another layer of complexity to branding. As brands expand into new markets, they must navigate diverse cultural landscapes while maintaining a consistent brand identity. This balancing act can be tricky, as what resonates in one culture may not have the same effect in another. Successful global brands often employ a strategy of localization, customizing their messaging and products to fit the preferences and values of each market. A great example is McDonald's, which adapts its menu to reflect local tastes while still keeping its core brand identity intact. This flexibility not only builds consumer trust but also shows a brand's commitment to understanding and respecting cultural differences.

Reflecting on the evolution of branding in light of cultural influences, it becomes clear that effectively navigating these changes requires a deep understanding of consumer values. Brands must proactively recognize societal shifts and be responsive in their messaging. By aligning with cultural movements and embracing sustainability, brands can forge strong connections with consumers that go beyond traditional marketing.

Looking ahead, the relationship between branding and consumers is more significant than ever. As we move from ancient branding practices to a modern landscape filled with digital interactions and cultural awareness, it's vital for consumers to think critically about their connections with brands. Understanding branding's ability to shape perceptions and influence choices empowers consumers to engage with the marketplace in a thoughtful way.

This exploration of branding shows its dual nature: it's a powerful marketing tool that enhances consumer choice, but it can also be a means of manipulation. By grasping branding's evolution and its implications, consumers can navigate today's marketplace with greater awareness, demanding transparency, authenticity, and accountability from the brands they choose to support. In the upcoming chapters, we'll dive deeper into the psychological, visual, and ethical dimensions of branding, offering insights that will further equip readers on their consumer journeys.

Lucas Sheffield

CHAPTER 2:
PSYCHOLOGICAL FOUNDATIONS

Branding is much more than just logos and catchy slogans; it delves into the rich and intricate world of human psychology. When we choose products and services, it's crucial to understand that our decisions are often influenced by factors we might not even realize. To highlight this, let's think about a relatable scenario.

Picture yourself stepping into a cozy coffee shop, the delightful smell of freshly brewed coffee filling the air. As you approach the counter, you see an array of choices: artisanal lattes, flavored cold brews, and classic espressos. Your gaze lands on a sleek black bottle of cold brew coffee, beautifully designed with minimalistic touches and an eye-catching logo. You've never tasted it before, but something about the brand name rings a bell—maybe it was featured in a trendy lifestyle magazine or endorsed by a celebrity you admire.

You decide to buy the bottle, and as you take your first sip, the rich flavor dances on your palate. But what if I told you that your enjoyment might be less about the taste and more about the branding that shaped your expectations? This illustrates the psychological impact of branding. The connection you form with that brand is emotional, created through marketing strategies meant to trigger specific feelings and attitudes.

We often overlook how subtly branding can sway our thoughts and emotions. This chapter aims to peel back the layers of understanding regarding how psychological factors—like the placebo effect, emotional triggers, and cognitive biases—shape our buying choices and brand perceptions. By diving into these psychological foundations, we can begin to grasp the significant influence brands have over our decisions, often without our awareness.

Let's start by looking at the placebo effect. Many people associate this term with the medical field, where it refers to when someone feels better from a treatment that has no real therapeutic value, simply because they believe it will work. Surprisingly, this effect extends beyond healthcare and into the world of consumer products.

In branding, the placebo effect shows us that consumers can feel a greater sense of satisfaction with a product just because of their perception of its brand. For example, there's a notable study in the pharmaceutical industry where patients taking a branded drug reported better results than those taking a generic one, even when both drugs contained the same active ingredient. The reputation of the brand and the imagery tied to it created trust and a sense of effectiveness, leading people to believe they were receiving superior care.

This psychological twist isn't just for medicines and health products. In the food industry, branding can significantly alter how consumers perceive taste. Research has shown that when people were given wine in unmarked bottles, they rated its flavor and quality much lower than when the same wine was served with a well-known label. The brand name influenced their expectations, changing how they experienced the product. This observation shows how branding can shape our beliefs and even alter our actual experiences, creating narratives that envelop consumers in a certain perception of reality.

Next, let's talk about emotional triggers. Brands don't just sell products; they sell connections and experiences. Successful branding often relies on the ability to evoke emotions that resonate with consumers personally. A powerful way brands do this is through storytelling, which not only engages consumers but helps create lasting memories.

Think about the emotional impact of holiday advertising campaigns. Each year, brands release commercials that tug at our heartstrings, often featuring themes like family gatherings, generosity, and love. One particularly memorable ad from a popular retail chain shows a family coming together around a beautifully set table for a festive meal. The warmth and joy depicted in the ad evoke nostalgia, causing viewers to associate those lovely feelings with the brand itself. This emotional connection can lead to consumer loyalty as individuals feel a deeper bond with the brand.

Moreover, brands often align themselves with social causes, further enhancing their emotional appeal. By positioning themselves as advocates for important issues, companies create a sense of shared values with consumers. For instance, a well-known outdoor clothing brand has built its identity around environmental conservation. Their campaigns highlight efforts like sustainable sourcing and community engagement, making consumers feel proud to support a brand that reflects their own values. This emotional bond can lead to strong brand loyalty, where customers become advocates themselves, sharing their positive experiences with others.

The relationship between emotion and branding isn't just about attracting customers; it also plays a vital role in keeping them loyal. When consumers feel a genuine connection to a brand, they're more likely to overlook its flaws, defend it in discussions, and stay loyal even when faced with alternatives. In a competitive marketplace, brands that successfully tap into emotional triggers have a clear edge.

As we continue to explore the psychological mechanisms in branding, we come to cognitive biases. Cognitive biases are patterns that lead people away from rational judgment and can cause them to make illogical conclusions. Brands have become skilled at using these biases to influence consumer decisions, boosting their attractiveness and driving sales.

One common example is confirmation bias, which is the tendency to seek out and interpret information that supports one's existing beliefs. Brands can take advantage of this bias by tailoring their messages to align with what their target audience already thinks or prefers. For example, if someone believes that organic products are healthier, a brand can reinforce this belief by emphasizing the organic aspects of its offerings. This strategy not only strengthens the consumer's attachment to the brand but also makes them likely to overlook any conflicting information that might challenge their views.

Another cognitive bias that brands skillfully manipulate is the anchoring effect. This occurs when people rely too heavily on the first piece of information they encounter when making decisions. Brands often use pricing tactics that illustrate this bias. For example, a product might be shown at a steep discount from a suggested retail price, anchoring consumers to that higher original price. By showcasing the perceived savings, brands create a sense of urgency and value, effectively nudging consumers toward a purchase. This tactic takes advantage of our natural tendency to cling to the first price we see, often leading us to believe we're getting a better deal than we actually are.

The bandwagon effect is another cognitive bias brands skillfully utilize. This happens when people adopt a belief or behavior simply because others are doing the same, creating a feeling of social pressure. Brands often flaunt their popularity through testimonials, social media followers, and user-generated content, encouraging consumers to join in. When potential buyers see that a product is widely accepted and endorsed by others, they're more likely to hop on the bandwagon, viewing the brand as trustworthy and desirable.

Research supports the idea that brands have finely tuned their understanding of cognitive biases to make their products more appealing. Studies show that consumers are more inclined to make impulsive purchases when faced with limited-time offers, effectively using both the anchoring effect and the bandwagon effect to spark urgency and excitement. In this light, branding acts as a catalyst for decision-making, guiding consumers toward choices that align with the brand's goals.

Throughout this chapter, we've examined the psychological foundations of branding, uncovering the intricate mechanisms that shape consumer behavior. From the placebo effect to emotional triggers and cognitive biases, it's clear that brands operate on a level that often escapes our conscious awareness, subtly molding our attitudes and actions. By understanding these psychological factors, we can navigate the marketplace with greater awareness, empowering ourselves to make informed decisions.

As we move forward, our exploration of branding will continue to reveal new dimensions and complexities, shedding light on how branding interacts with consumer psychology. By becoming more aware of these psychological influences, we can engage more thoughtfully with the brands that surround us, ensuring we remain informed and discerning consumers in a constantly changing marketplace. Brand perception and identity are vital pieces of the branding puzzle, deeply influencing how consumers behave. When we look closer at how these elements interact, it becomes clear that the way people view brands significantly affects their identities and buying choices. A term you might hear often in marketing is brand equity. This refers to the value a brand brings to a product or service and often enables companies to charge higher prices. When a brand has a strong and meaningful presence, consumers are willing to spend more—not just on the product itself, but also for the status and sense of identity that comes with it.

Let's think about some of the iconic brands that have nailed their identities: Apple, Nike, and Coca-Cola. Each of these brands tells a unique story that connects with consumers on different levels. For example, Apple isn't just a tech company; it represents innovation, creativity, and a specific lifestyle. The sleek look, simple design, and easy-to-use products create an image that attracts people who see themselves as forward-thinking and creative. When someone chooses an Apple product, they often make a statement about who they are, aligning themselves with the values that Apple stands for.

Nike, on the other hand, has positioned itself as a symbol of athleticism, determination, and excellence. The famous "Just Do It" slogan goes beyond traditional marketing; it resonates with consumers who aspire to achieve greatness, whether in sports or in life. By connecting with successful athletes and sharing inspiring stories of perseverance, Nike has built a strong emotional bond with its audience. When consumers sport a pair of Nike shoes or wear a hoodie with its logo, they aren't just purchasing athletic gear; they are embracing a mindset tied to success and resilience.

Coca-Cola is another brand that has mastered the art of connection through its timeless branding strategies. It has established itself as the go-to beverage that brings people together. The brand's marketing often revolves around shared experiences and happiness, embedding Coca-

Cola into cultural moments—from holiday celebrations to summer barbecues. For many, drinking a Coke evokes feelings of nostalgia and cherished memories, reinforcing a sense of belonging. This emotional attachment helps build loyalty, as people are drawn to brands that reflect their values and desired identities.

As consumers navigate their choices, they look for brands that resonate with their personal values, goals, and identities. This creates a strong link between branding and self-perception. When someone aligns with a brand that reflects their ideal self, it not only boosts their self-image but also builds loyalty to that brand. This loyalty can be so profound that it leads to communities forming around specific brands, where individuals feel connected with others who share their enthusiasm.

However, it's essential to consider the ethical aspects that come into play in the branding world. With the power to shape identities comes the responsibility to do so ethically. Branding can have positive effects—like promoting healthier lifestyles, encouraging community engagement, and supporting social causes—but it can also lead to manipulation. Marketers have a strong influence over consumer behavior, and the strategies they employ can sometimes blur ethical lines.

Take the health food industry, for example. Many brands advertise their products by emphasizing health benefits, tapping into consumers' desires for better well-being. While this can be beneficial, there's also the risk of manipulation. Brands might exaggerate claims or use deceptive marketing tactics to create the illusion that their products are much healthier than others. This not only misleads consumers but also preys on their insecurities about health, pushing them toward choices that may not be in their best interest.

A notable example of this manipulation occurred in the late 1990s and early 2000s when many food brands began labeling their products as "fat-free" or "low-fat." In reality, these items were often filled with sugar or artificial ingredients to make up for the flavor lost when fat was removed. Consumers, drawn in by the promise of healthier options, flocked to these products, believing they were making smart choices. This created a cycle of confusion, as people struggled to understand what healthy eating truly meant. It illustrates the ethical tension between marketing tactics and consumer well-being, where the chase for profit can overshadow the duty to inform and educate.

Reflecting on the ethical implications of branding, it's crucial for consumers to develop a critical awareness of the marketing messages they encounter every day. Understanding the psychological tactics brands use can empower individuals to make informed choices. This involves recognizing emotional triggers and cognitive biases, and questioning the motives behind branding strategies. Consumers should consider whether the brands they support genuinely align with their values or if they are merely responding to clever marketing.

Taking a step back and analyzing these dynamics can help consumers navigate this tricky landscape with confidence. They can reflect on their motivations for purchasing certain brands. Are they seeking social acceptance, or do their choices truly align with the brand's values? This self-reflection is key to becoming a savvy consumer.

As we bring this chapter to a close, it's a good time to think about the subtle ways our interactions with brands can shape us. By understanding the psychological elements we've discussed—like emotional triggers, cognitive biases, and ethical considerations—we can begin to see the complex nature of our consumer behavior. It's important to stress that gaining this understanding isn't just an academic exercise; it has real consequences for how we engage with the marketplace.

Branding itself isn't inherently good or bad; it's simply a tool that can be used for both positive and negative results. When consumers are knowledgeable, they empower themselves to recognize genuine value versus potential manipulation. This awareness allows them to make choices that resonate with their true selves, fostering a deeper and more authentic connection with the brands they choose to support.

As we close this chapter, we should keep in mind that the relationship between consumers and brands is always changing. It evolves as societal values shift and as consumers become more aware of the impact of their choices. Today's consumers are more informed and connected than ever before, seeking transparency and authenticity in the brands they support. This ongoing evolution requires brands to rethink how they communicate and engage with their audiences.

Through engaging storytelling, thorough research, and thoughtful analysis, this chapter sets the stage for deeper discussions in the following chapters. It invites consumers to take an active role in the branding narrative, shaping their identities through mindful choices rather than passive consumption. By fostering this informed consumer base, we can create an environment where brands thrive while also encouraging positive consumer behavior and ethical practices. As we move forward into the next chapters, this foundational understanding will be an essential guide, helping readers grasp the significant role branding plays in their lives.

Lucas Sheffield

CHAPTER 3: THE VISUAL LANGUAGE OF BRANDING

When it comes to branding, the role of visuals is absolutely crucial. They act as the first point of contact between a brand and its audience, conveying messages that can resonate with consumers long before they even consider purchasing a product. For many people, a brand is more than just a name or a product; it's an experience, heavily influenced by the visual aspects surrounding it. Thoughtful design choices—like logos, color schemes, and packaging—are essential to shaping how consumers perceive and interact with brands. These elements are key for any brand looking to make a strong impression in the market.

Let's take a moment to think about first impressions. Often, these impressions are formed in mere seconds, driven primarily by what we see. Studies have shown that it only takes about 10 seconds for someone to form an opinion about a brand after their first encounter. This highlights the power of a brand's visual identity, which includes its colors, logos, and overall design. A strong visual identity can boost brand recognition, stir emotions, and build lasting connections with consumers.

Color psychology is one of the most fascinating aspects of branding. Different colors can convey various messages and feelings, and they often trigger specific emotional responses in consumers. For example, blue is frequently linked to trust, reliability, and professionalism. That's why you'll see many financial institutions and tech companies, like American Express and IBM, prominently feature blue in their branding. This creates an atmosphere of safety and dependability in the minds of their customers.

On the flip side, warmer colors like red and yellow tend to spark feelings of excitement and urgency. Fast food restaurants such as McDonald's and Burger King use these colors to stimulate appetites and encourage quick decisions. The bright red of McDonald's logo grabs attention and makes people feel hungry, pushing them towards making a purchase. The golden arches of McDonald's also radiate warmth and happiness, creating an inviting space for families and children.

It's also essential to recognize that the emotional connections tied to colors can differ from one culture to another, adding complexity to visual branding. For example, while white is often seen as a symbol of purity and peace in many Western cultures, it can represent mourning in some Eastern societies. This illustrates why understanding cultural contexts is so important for brands aiming to reach diverse audiences. By being aware of how colors are perceived in different cultures, brands can tailor their visual identities to better connect with their target consumers.

Moving past color, logos act as a shorthand for brands. A logo can encapsulate a brand's identity and values in a single image, making it a powerful tool for recognition and recall. Take McDonald's golden arches, for instance; they have become almost synonymous with fast food and family dining. Many people instantly recognize this logo, and it often brings back feelings of nostalgia, transcending language and cultural barriers. The design of this logo—its simplicity, prominence, and color choices—ensures that it stays memorable and impactful.

The Nike swoosh offers another great example of effective logo design. This simple checkmark carries a lot of meaning; it embodies movement, speed, and agility, perfectly aligning with the brand's focus on athleticism and performance. The swoosh represents more than just a logo; it stands for a mindset—striving for excellence in sports. The emotional bond consumers have with this logo often leads to brand loyalty, as people are inspired by the aspirations that Nike promotes.

Logos tell stories, too. Many brands utilize storytelling in their branding, and logos often serve as the starting point for these narratives. A logo's backstory can deepen a consumer's emotional connection to the brand. For instance, the evolution of the Apple logo reflects the company's journey from a small tech startup to a global leader in innovation. It began with a depiction of Sir Isaac Newton sitting under an apple tree, transforming into the minimalist apple we recognize today—a symbol of simplicity, creativity, and cutting-edge technology.

As we look at the strategic role of visuals in branding, it's clear that they are more than just decorative elements; they are foundational to a brand's identity. Packaging design is another vital aspect that often goes unnoticed. Packaging does more than house a product; it acts as a canvas for storytelling and brand expression. Well-crafted packaging can grab attention on crowded shelves, convey product quality, and reinforce brand values.

Take high-end cosmetics, for example. Brands like Estée Lauder and Chanel pour significant resources into designing their product containers, ensuring that every detail—from the materials to the color palette—exudes luxury and sophistication. Elegant glass bottles adorned with minimalist logos not only protect the product inside but also tell a captivating story of beauty and exclusivity. This thoughtful packaging can evoke emotions, enticing consumers to indulge in the experience of using these premium products.

Visual branding is about more than just attractive designs; it also builds consumer trust and loyalty. When customers see a brand consistently presented in its visuals, it fosters a sense of reliability. Consistency in branding—through colors, typography, or logo design—helps consumers easily recognize and recall a brand across various platforms. This recognition is crucial for nurturing long-term relationships with customers.

Research indicates that consumers are more inclined to engage with brands that maintain a cohesive visual identity. If a brand's visuals vary significantly across different platforms, it can lead to confusion and erode trust. For example, if a company's website uses a color palette that starkly contrasts with its social media profiles, consumers might question its credibility. A steady visual identity strengthens a brand's standing in the marketplace and ultimately contributes to customer loyalty.

In crafting a strong visual identity, brands must also pay attention to the trends that influence what consumers expect. In today's fast-paced digital world, where attention spans are short and competition is fierce, minimalist design has become a favorite. Brands that adopt a clean, uncluttered look often succeed in grabbing consumer interest. This trend reflects a broader societal movement towards simplicity and authenticity, as people increasingly connect with brands that share their values.

However, it's crucial to remember that branding isn't just about following trends; it's also about being genuine. A brand's visual identity should align with its mission, values, and the experiences it promises. For example, outdoor brands like Patagonia use earthy tones and rugged designs to highlight their commitment to environmental sustainability. The choices they make in their visuals resonate with consumers who value authenticity and responsibility, fostering a deeper connection that goes beyond just aesthetics.

As we dive deeper into how visual elements influence branding, we must also consider the ethical implications of shaping perceptions. While visual branding can enhance consumer experiences and build loyalty, it can also lead to misleading practices. For instance, brands that exaggerate through packaging or color choices can leave consumers feeling betrayed when the product doesn't meet expectations.

In a world where consumers are becoming more savvy about branding tactics, transparency and honesty are essential. Brands that take ethical considerations seriously in their visual branding efforts tend to gain trust and goodwill among their audiences. By staying genuine in their messaging and visual representations, brands can establish a solid foundation for lasting relationships with consumers.

To sum it all up, visual elements in branding go far beyond mere decorations; they play a crucial role in shaping how consumers perceive and respond to a brand. From the colors that stir emotions to logos that capture a brand's essence, these elements create a powerful language that speaks to consumers on a deeper level. As branding continues to evolve, recognizing the importance of these visual elements will empower consumers to navigate the marketplace with greater awareness, helping them make informed choices that align with their values and preferences.

When it comes to branding, the design of packaging plays a vital role. It acts as a key link between the consumer and the product, often being the last thing someone interacts with before deciding to buy. As shoppers weave through aisles packed with countless items, the design of packaging can be what first grabs their attention. It's more than just looking good; packaging reflects a brand's identity and communicates its values in just a fleeting moment. In this section, we'll explore how brands skillfully use different aspects of packaging to create a memorable and convincing experience for shoppers.

Let's start with the materials used in packaging. A brand that focuses on sustainability might use recyclable materials, sending a strong message about its dedication to protecting the environment. For example, think about a luxurious skincare line that chooses frosted glass instead of plastic for its containers. This choice not only screams luxury and elegance, but it also ties into a larger conversation about sustainability and quality. The feel of glass, its weight, and its gleam give an immediate impression of high quality, often suggesting that the product inside is top-notch too. This isn't just surface-level;

research in consumer psychology shows that how people perceive quality is heavily influenced by the sensory experience of packaging.

Next, let's consider the shape of the packaging. The famous contour bottle of Coca-Cola is a perfect example. This unique shape isn't just practical; it's become closely tied to the brand itself, creating a visual cue that people recognize instantly. Brands like Coca-Cola know that a distinctive shape can spark curiosity and build loyalty among customers. On the other hand, many everyday products, like household cleaners, tend to have simple and straightforward designs. While these designs may be clear and functional, they often lack the emotional connection that a unique shape can foster.

Color is another crucial element of packaging design. Brands carefully select color schemes to evoke specific emotions. Bright and lively colors are often found in candy packaging, appealing to children and creating a sense of joy and excitement. Conversely, muted and elegant tones in luxury brand packaging speak to adults, suggesting exclusivity and refined taste. Research in color psychology indicates that colors can significantly impact how we feel and how we perceive things, ultimately affecting whether or not we decide to buy. For instance, studies show that reds and yellows can stimulate appetite, which is why you often see these colors in fast-food marketing aimed at attracting hungry customers.

Now, let's shift our focus to the bigger picture of visual storytelling in branding. Nowadays, brands aren't just selling products; they're creating experiences and telling stories that resonate with their target audiences. This approach is crucial in a market overflowing with choices. Take Apple, for instance. Their marketing doesn't just highlight the product; it emphasizes sleek visuals, aspirational lifestyles, and innovation. In Apple's ads, it's not just about the gadget itself but the experience of using it—connecting with people on an emotional level. For many, owning an Apple product is about more than practicality; it's a status symbol and a reflection of their identity.

The storytelling aspect of branding goes beyond just listing product features. It embodies the entire spirit of the brand. The visuals in Apple's marketing convey not just the sophistication of their technology but also an aspirational lifestyle that many people aspire to. As a result, consumers often feel a personal connection to the brand, believing they belong to an exclusive community that values innovation, creativity, and modernity. This bond can be incredibly strong, leading to lasting loyalty.

Similarly, Coca-Cola has mastered the art of visual storytelling. Many of its advertisements capture moments filled with togetherness, nostalgia, and joy. By showcasing people sharing a Coke during special moments, the brand positions itself as a staple in life's celebrations. Many individuals have personal stories about how Coca-Cola has been part of family traditions or memorable events. This emotional connection transforms a simple drink into a cherished brand that feels special to millions.

However, as we explore the influence of visual branding, it's crucial to consider the ethical implications that come with these strategies. With great influence comes great responsibility, and the line between persuasion and manipulation can be dangerously thin. While effective visual branding can enrich consumer experiences, it can also lead to exploitation, particularly among vulnerable groups who may be more susceptible to misleading advertising.

Think about brands that have faced criticism for using deceptive packaging tactics. One well-known case involved a popular snack brand that used bright colors and playful graphics to attract children while claiming health benefits for its products. Parents were outraged to learn that the ingredients were not as healthy as the packaging suggested. This incident raised serious concerns about the ethics of focusing marketing efforts on children through visually appealing tactics that prioritize looks and sales over honesty and transparency.

The ethical challenges don't stop with children. Adults can also fall victim to manipulative branding. For example, a brand might package a product in a way that suggests it's of higher quality than it actually is, using design elements that create an illusion of premium value. This practice harms consumer trust and raises questions about corporate responsibility. Consumers deserve transparency, especially when it comes to choices that affect their health and well-being.

As you think back on your own experiences as a consumer, you'll likely remember times when branding influenced your decisions—sometimes positively, but at other times, misleadingly. Developing the ability to recognize when a brand's visual presentation is just for show as opposed to when it's meant to deceive is a valuable skill in today's marketplace. By cultivating a critical perspective, consumers can better navigate branding strategies.

As we dig into the complex dynamics of visual branding, it's clear that design elements are not just for decoration; they play a crucial role in shaping the consumer experience. From the materials and shapes to the colors and the stories they tell, every aspect significantly influences our perceptions and behaviors. The relationship between a brand and its consumers is intricate, woven with emotions, values, and social narratives.

By diving into how design affects our perceptions and choices, we hope to give you a deeper understanding of the profound impact that visual branding has on consumer behavior and the marketplace as a whole. This chapter encourages you to look at visual marketing with a critical eye, acknowledging both the power of branding and the ethical considerations that come along with it. In a world overflowing with options and information at our fingertips, a well-informed and discerning approach to branding will help you navigate the complexities of consumerism with confidence.

Lucas Sheffield

CHAPTER 4: THE POWER OF NAMES AND SYMBOLS

What makes a name stick in our minds? How do symbols tap into our emotions and memories? These questions swirl around the fascinating world of branding, where every name and logo carries its own set of meanings and feelings. Think back to the first time you encountered a brand that really caught your attention. Maybe it was the crisp, refreshing taste of a Coca-Cola, coupled with its eye-catching red logo that pulled you in, or the iconic swoosh of Nike—a symbol that seems to embody energy and movement. Every day, we interact with these brands, often without even noticing the deeper psychological and historical threads that lie beneath our everyday choices.

Branding is woven into the very fabric of our lives, guiding our decisions and shaping how we see the world. Unbeknownst to us, each time we buy something, we are also expressing the identity we want to show to others. This chapter will dive into the significant roles that names and symbols play in our decisions, drawing on historical examples, psychological insights, and engaging case studies that show how branding impacts consumer behavior.

Looking back in history, names and symbols have roots that go all the way back to the dawn of trade. In ancient societies, symbols were vital for establishing trust and identity among merchants. For example, in ancient Greece, traders displayed unique logos to indicate their products, ensuring that buyers could recognize the quality and origin of what they were purchasing. These early branding efforts were crucial in a time when word-of-mouth was key, and having a good reputation was everything. Similarly, during the medieval era, guilds used symbols to represent their craftsmanship, helping consumers understand the skill behind the products they were buying. These practices laid the groundwork for today's branding landscape, where names and symbols not only identify a brand but also tell a story that reflects its mission and values.

As time moved on, branding grew more complex. Names began to take on richer meanings, often designed to spark specific feelings or associations. This evolution isn't just about the words we use; it involves the psychological insights that shape how we connect with brands. Research in psychology has uncovered interesting findings about our relationships with names and symbols. One example is the "name-letter effect," which suggests that people tend to favor brands that include letters from their own names. This curious phenomenon suggests a deeper psychological bond that influences how we perceive brands, highlighting how names can resonate with our sense of self.

Additionally, the way we learn through association plays a key role in how we view brands. As consumers, we often tie positive emotions and experiences to certain brands, creating complex networks of associations that guide our buying habits. For instance, a memorable advertisement featuring a favorite celebrity can leave a lasting impression, blending the brand with feelings of happiness, success, or aspiration. In this way, names and symbols act as gateways for emotional expression, reminding us of personal experiences and shared cultural stories.

To showcase the powerful influence of names and symbols in branding, let's take a look at Nike. Its famous swoosh is more than just a logo; it symbolizes athletic excellence and achievement. The sleek and dynamic design of this logo captures the brand's spirit perfectly, resonating with consumers who aspire to achieve greatness in their lives. Over the years, Nike has skillfully harnessed the emotional impact of the swoosh in its marketing, often featuring athletes who embody the drive and determination that the brand represents. Customers often share how the swoosh inspires them, showing just how impactful a symbol can be in shaping our connections to a brand.

On a different note, we have Coca-Cola, a brand that has successfully navigated the shifting landscape of consumer preferences with remarkable finesse. The journey of Coca-Cola's name and logo is a textbook example of adaptive branding. Originally called "Pemberton's French Wine Coca," the drink transformed into one of the most recognized names in the world. Over the years, Coca-Cola has made smart choices that respond to changing consumer demands, showing how important it is to adapt in the world of branding. From its classic cursive font to its bold red and white color scheme, the brand has effectively kept its identity while evolving to remain relevant in a competitive market.

Both Nike and Coca-Cola are powerful examples of how names and symbols can shape what consumers think and how they act. Their stories reveal the delicate balance between historical roots and modern reinvention, and how the psychology of branding influences our relationships with these iconic companies. As we continue on this journey, we'll uncover more case studies that shed light on the dynamic interplay between branding, consumer psychology, and market trends, helping us recognize the subtle influences that shape our everyday purchasing choices.

In our exploration of names and symbols, we will aim to uncover not only their historical importance but also their psychological effects on consumer behavior. By examining these aspects, we will empower ourselves to engage more thoughtfully with brands, improving our decision-making processes when we shop. Each name we see and every symbol we recognize carries layers of meaning that can guide our choices, whether we're picking out a new pair of sneakers or grabbing a refreshing drink on a hot summer day.

As we move forward in this exploration, we'll reflect on how branding has evolved over the years, mirroring changes in society and consumer expectations. We'll examine how brands have adapted to cultural shifts and technological advances, and how these changes influence how we perceive and interact with them. By doing this, we'll appreciate the essential role branding plays in our lives—not just as a means of commerce, but as part of the story that shapes our identities and experiences in a complex world.

By grasping the intricate nature of branding, we can navigate the marketplace with greater awareness, making informed choices that align with our values and aspirations. While branding can sway our decisions, it's ultimately up to us as consumers to engage with it thoughtfully, discerning the motives behind the names and symbols that fill our everyday lives. In the chapters ahead, we'll keep exploring this fascinating relationship, uncovering more dimensions of branding that highlight its significance in shaping our modern marketplace. Apple's branding strategy serves as an impressive example of how simplicity and symbolism can create a powerful impact. The minimalist style Apple uses in its marketing and product design isn't just about looking good; it's a thoughtful choice that embodies innovation, exclusivity, and top-tier quality. The well-known apple symbol, with its clean design and straightforward look, sparks feelings of both comfort and aspiration. Over the years, this emblem has come to represent cutting-edge technology and the lifestyle many people dream of, creating a strong emotional bond between the brand and its followers.

Apple has crafted a brand identity that goes much deeper than just selling gadgets. It promotes a lifestyle that feels modern, sophisticated, and forward-thinking. Their messaging often centers on empowerment—encouraging users to express their creativity, connect in innovative ways, and enhance their lives through technology. This idea shines through in their advertising campaigns, product launches, and even the layout of Apple Stores. These stores are inviting spaces designed for exploration and interaction. Buying an Apple product is not just about making a purchase; it feels like a special event, strengthening the emotional ties customers have with the brand.

      The loyalty that consumers show towards Apple is fascinating and highlights the deep psychological connections that branding can create. Many Apple users exhibit a level of enthusiasm for the brand that is almost fanatical—eagerly anticipating the latest product announcements and camping outside stores for days to be among the first to get their hands on the newest iPhone or MacBook. This intense loyalty can be traced back to several reasons, including Apple's consistent delivery of high-quality products, the aspirational lifestyle they promote, and the community that surrounds the brand. By aligning itself with values like creativity, individuality, and innovation, Apple has managed to position itself not just as a tech company but as a cultural icon that resonates deeply with its consumers.

On the flip side, we see Target's bullseye symbol, which stands for accessibility and inclusivity. Target has created a niche for itself as a retailer that offers stylish yet affordable products. The bullseye is a strong visual marker that conveys the brand's promise of quality without the hefty price tag. Unlike brands that may feel exclusive, Target's branding invites everyone in, encouraging customers to explore and enjoy the shopping experience without the stress of overspending.

Target's marketing campaigns often highlight community and family values, making them relatable to a wide audience. By presenting itself as an accessible brand, Target nurtures a sense of belonging among shoppers. The emotional connection consumers feel towards Target isn't just about transactions; it's rooted in the idea that Target is a friendly brand that understands their needs and preferences. This connection is especially evident during key shopping seasons, like back-to-school or the holidays, when Target's branding evokes feelings of warmth, nostalgia, and togetherness.

When we look deeper into branding and its cultural and emotional significance, it's clear that names and symbols play a crucial role in shaping how consumers perceive products. Take McDonald's, for example. This global brand has developed various branding strategies to connect with different cultural contexts. While the golden arches are recognized around the world, McDonald's often tailors its menu and marketing to suit local tastes and customs. In India, for instance, they offer a variety of vegetarian options to respect cultural preferences, while in the Middle East, they adhere to halal dietary guidelines. This flexibility shows how important it is for brands to be culturally aware, allowing them to grow while honoring local traditions.

Symbols can also stir powerful emotions that cross geographical boundaries. A logo or brand name might evoke memories for one person while representing modernity for another. Understanding the emotional undercurrents of branding is essential—it's not just about creating a catchy slogan or eye-catching logo; it's about tapping into the feelings and perceptions of the target audience. Brands that succeed in establishing this emotional connection often build a loyal customer base that feels a deeper bond with the brand.

As consumers navigate their choices, it's important to approach brand perceptions thoughtfully. Companies are constantly competing for attention with a variety of marketing tactics, which can make it tough to identify what truly offers value. To help readers cut through the noise, it's essential to provide tools and strategies for evaluating brands critically. Breaking down key branding elements—like the name, logo, colors, and messaging—can be a great start. Questions such as "What feelings does this brand stir in me?" or "How does this brand fit with my values?" can help consumers reflect on their thoughts and feelings about different brands.

Self-reflection is key in understanding how branding influences buying choices. By recognizing personal feelings and the weight that brands carry, shoppers can make more informed decisions. Discussing branding with friends or family can also deepen this understanding, as sharing perspectives can uncover insights or viewpoints that one might not have considered on their own.

As readers dive further into the complex world of branding, it becomes evident that names and symbols hold significant power. They are more than just marketing tools; they shape identities, build connections, and subtly influence consumer behavior. The path to becoming a thoughtful consumer involves recognizing the nuances of branding and understanding how it impacts personal choices.

By embracing this awareness, readers can navigate the branding landscape with confidence and clarity. With a better understanding of how branding works and the emotional ties it creates, consumers can interact with products and services more thoughtfully. This not only improves their shopping experiences but also fosters a deeper understanding of their own consumption habits.

As we wrap up this look into branding, it's important to emphasize the value of being an informed consumer. The intricate relationship between branding, consumer behavior, and cultural dynamics presents a wealth of opportunities for exploration and thought. Readers are encouraged to stay curious, question their perceptions, and seek out brands that resonate authentically with their values and identities. By doing this, they'll not only make better choices but also help promote a marketplace that values transparency, inclusivity, and genuine connection.

Lucas Sheffield

CHAPTER 5: THE POWER OF SOCIAL PROOF IN BRANDING

Social proof is a fascinating idea that has caught the attention of both psychologists and marketers. It refers to how the behavior and opinions of others can influence our decisions, especially when we're not sure what to do. When faced with choices, we often turn to the actions of our peers for guidance. This is especially true in branding, as social proof acts as a powerful tool for shaping how we shop and what we think about different products. Its importance in modern marketing is clear; it plays a key role in what we buy, who we trust, and how we feel about brands.

Let's start by looking at the Bandwagon Effect. This psychological phenomenon explains why people are more likely to adopt certain behaviors or beliefs when they see others doing the same thing. Think back to a time when you were scrolling through social media and came across a post about a product that had "gone viral." Maybe it was a cool new gadget or a fashionable item that everyone seemed to be talking about. In those moments, the desire to fit in can push consumers to make spur-of-the-moment purchases, driven by a wish to align themselves with what appears to be trendy or desirable. The Bandwagon Effect shows that people are more likely to hop on the bandwagon of a popular product once they see others embracing it with excitement.

Social Proof Theory goes even further by illustrating how we often look to social cues to determine whether an action or belief is valid. This is especially common in uncertain situations where we might not have enough information to make a well-informed choice. For example, if you walk into a new restaurant and notice it's packed while the one next door is nearly empty, chances are you'll choose the bustling spot. The crowd serves as a form of validation, suggesting that the busy restaurant must be the better choice. Similarly, in shopping, the preferences and endorsements of others can significantly steer our buying decisions.

To showcase the strong impact of social proof, let's look at a few real-life examples. One notable story is about a popular beverage brand that saw its sales skyrocket after a viral social media campaign. This brand introduced a unique drink aimed at a niche market, but it was relatively unknown until a major influencer posted about it. Suddenly, the product was in the spotlight. Comments rolled in as people expressed their eagerness to try it, share their experiences, and imitate the influencer's lifestyle. Almost overnight, stores struggled to keep the drink in stock due to the surge in demand. This situation perfectly illustrates how social proof, amplified through digital channels, can propel a brand to new heights.

Another compelling example comes from a well-known cosmetics company. They had traditionally relied on standard advertising, but their sales growth had plateaued. Realizing they needed a fresh approach, they decided to harness social proof by encouraging customers to share their makeup looks using a specific hashtag.

This campaign fostered a sense of community among users and allowed potential buyers to see the products in action, applied by real people instead of just models in glossy ads. The result? Sales skyrocketed as consumers felt more connected to the brand and more confident in their purchasing decisions, having witnessed the positive experiences of others.

Now, let's take a closer look at customer testimonials, one of the most effective tools brands can use to boost credibility. In a world where many consumers are skeptical of marketing messages, testimonials provide genuine voices that resonate with potential buyers. These endorsements can come in many forms, from written reviews on e-commerce sites to video testimonials shared on social media. Each type serves to validate the brand and its offerings, reinforcing the idea that good experiences can lead to real benefits.

Consider the rise of review websites like Yelp, TripAdvisor, and Amazon. User-generated content has changed how consumers connect with brands. Research shows that consumers trust peer reviews much more than traditional advertising; in fact, a significant number of people report reading reviews before making a purchase. This change in trust dynamics highlights the importance of leveraging social proof through customer testimonials and demonstrates the powerful influence it can have on buying behavior.

Let's dive into a specific case study to highlight this point further. A home goods retailer encouraged customers to leave reviews after their purchases. This approach not only led to a flood of testimonials but also built a sense of trust and community among shoppers. The retailer prominently displayed these reviews on their website and social media, carefully placing them to sway potential buyers at crucial moments in their shopping process. The result was impressive: a marked increase in conversion rates, with customers feeling more confident in their choices. By amplifying the voices of satisfied customers, the brand successfully used social proof to enhance its credibility and drive sales.

The psychology behind why consumers trust peer reviews more than brand messages lies in social validation. When we see others happy with a product or service, it creates not just trust but also a sense of belonging. We want to align ourselves with the social norms set by others, especially those whose opinions matter to us. This need for validation can lead to what's known as the "herd mentality," where consumers gravitate toward products that appear to be endorsed by their peers. Data shows that a substantial number of consumers base their purchasing decisions on feedback from others, underlining the crucial role testimonials play in branding.

Building on the foundation of customer testimonials, let's discuss celebrity endorsements as another powerful form of social proof. Celebrities, because of their fame and visibility, can captivate and influence large audiences. This trend isn't new; brands have been leveraging celebrity endorsements for decades, crafting partnerships that resonate with consumers on a deep level. When a famous person backs a product, it often creates an aspirational connection, elevating the brand's status and desirability.

Take the iconic partnership between Nike and Michael Jordan, for instance. This collaboration didn't just change the athletic shoe industry; it set a new gold standard for how brands could use celebrity endorsements. The Air Jordan line became synonymous with basketball excellence, and consumers weren't just buying shoes; they were investing in a lifestyle. Through this partnership, Nike tapped into the aspirational side of branding, allowing consumers to feel part of a larger narrative that went beyond mere footwear. The impact of this endorsement was clear—sales soared, and the brand's reputation was solidified in the market.

However, while celebrity endorsements can enhance a brand's image and credibility, it's crucial to recognize the potential risks that come with such partnerships. One major concern is the chance of alienating consumers who don't identify with the celebrity. If a brand teams up with a celebrity whose image doesn't align with its values, it could confuse or upset its target audience. This disconnect might lead to a backlash, where consumers feel the brand has strayed from its true identity. Therefore, brands need to think carefully about the implications of their celebrity partnerships, ensuring that the individuals they choose to work with resonate with their core values and the consumers they want to reach.

As we navigate the complex world of branding, understanding the different forms of social proof is essential. The effects of testimonials and celebrity endorsements reveal just how much others can influence our choices and perceptions. As we explore more examples and case studies in the upcoming sections, we'll uncover the dynamics at play, giving you a clearer picture of how these elements shape consumer behavior. The world of branding has changed dramatically in recent years, thanks in large part to the rise of social media influencers. These individuals have become powerful voices for consumers, often seen as more relatable and genuine than traditional celebrities. They engage directly with their followers, transforming the way brands connect with their target audiences. As we look closer at this trend, we start to see how influencer marketing plays into a fundamental psychological concept: social proof. By understanding how influencers work within this frame, we can truly grasp their effect on consumer behavior.

The journey of influencer marketing began with the early days of social media, where platforms like Instagram, YouTube, and TikTok enabled everyday people to grow large followings based on their interests and lifestyles. Unlike conventional celebrities, influencers often feel more approachable and relatable to their audiences. This sense of authenticity can be both a blessing and a curse. While it allows brands to tap into the strong connections influencers have with their followers, it also raises ethical questions about these partnerships.

A powerful example of influencer marketing at work is the collaboration between fashion brands and influencers who share their unique takes on style. Picture a well-known clothing brand teaming up with a fashion influencer who has millions of fans. The influencer showcases the brand's clothing through carefully designed posts and stories that feel natural and genuine. Instead of just being hit with ads, audiences are drawn into a narrative where the clothes seem like a vital part of their lives. This approach not only boosted sales but also created a sense of community among followers, making them feel like they were part of something bigger.

Influencers have a knack for reaching niche markets that traditional advertising often misses. By sharing their personal stories and insights, they create content that resonates with specific groups of people. Think of influencers focusing on sustainable fashion, vegan cooking, or budget travel— each of them carving out their own unique space in the market. Through these connections, they build strong relationships with their followers, who come to trust their recommendations. This bond is essential for the success of influencer marketing, as consumers often turn to their favorite influencers for advice when making purchasing decisions, viewing their opinions as a form of social proof that the products are worth considering.

However, as influencer marketing evolves, the ethical aspects surrounding it are coming under scrutiny. One major concern is transparency. The Federal Trade Commission (FTC) in the U.S. has guidelines requiring influencers to disclose any sponsored content. Unfortunately, not all influencers follow these rules, leading to confusion about what is real and what is not. When followers don't know about an influencer's financial ties to a product, the trust that forms the basis of the influencer-consumer relationship can easily be broken.

The issue of undisclosed sponsorships raises important questions about the authenticity of influencer promotions. Does receiving payment for an endorsement make an influencer's recommendation less genuine? For example, when an influencer, who usually promotes a frugal lifestyle, suddenly endorses a luxury brand, how does that affect their credibility? These are vital questions that we must consider as we navigate the changing world of influencer marketing.

To make matters more complicated, some brands participate in practices that artificially inflate social proof through manipulated endorsements or fake testimonials. There have been cases where brands create fake accounts to leave positive reviews or hire actors to pretend to be happy customers. These actions are not just unethical; they undermine the trust that is the bedrock of influencer marketing. When consumers realize they've been misled, it can lead to frustration and disappointment, not only with the brand but with influencer marketing as a whole.

As we ponder the ethical responsibilities brands have when using endorsements and testimonials, it's crucial to engage with different ethical perspectives to evaluate the morality of manipulating social proof for profit. For instance, Kantian ethics, which stresses honesty and integrity, would strongly oppose any practice involving deceit. Manipulating how consumers see a product for financial gain goes against this principle and can lead to long-lasting negative consequences for both brands and influencers.

On the flip side, a utilitarian viewpoint might argue that if a manipulated endorsement brings more happiness or satisfaction to most consumers, it could be justified. However, this perspective falls short when we consider the potential harm caused to those who feel deceived by false representations. This highlights the importance of brands prioritizing ethical considerations over quick profits, understanding that once consumer trust is lost, it's incredibly hard to regain.

Bringing in insights from marketing experts and ethicists adds even more depth to this discussion. Many in the industry stress how important it is to build authentic relationships between brands and influencers. When brands partner with influencers who truly align with their values, the resulting connection feels more real to consumers. The focus shouldn't just be on selling products but rather on creating a bond that fosters loyalty and trust.

As we examine the intricate relationship between social proof and authority in branding, it's increasingly essential for consumers to reflect on their own habits and the influences that shape their choices. Social proof is a powerful tool, but it can easily be manipulated, leading to a landscape where authenticity can feel scarce. Taking a moment to think critically about the sources of information and the motivations behind endorsements can empower consumers to navigate this ever-changing marketplace more wisely.

Reflecting on the main ideas of this chapter, it's clear that social proof and authority are crucial in the branding world. Understanding these concepts helps consumers recognize both the benefits and possible downsides of influencer marketing. So, as we wrap up this discussion, I invite you to think about your own experiences with social proof in branding. Have you ever been influenced by an endorsement from an influencer? How did it shape your purchasing choices? By sharing your stories and joining in on this conversation, we can create a community that understands the complexities of our consumer habits.

As we move on to the next chapter, which will explore the ethical dimensions of branding in the digital age, let's carry forward the insights we've gained about influence and consumer behavior. The digital landscape is changing quickly, and understanding the ethical responsibilities involved in branding will be more important than ever as we tackle the challenges that lie ahead. Let's continue this journey together, committed to fostering authenticity and integrity in our interactions with brands and influencers alike.

CHAPTER 6: THE POWER OF SCARCITY AND URGENCY IN BRANDING

Scarcity and urgency aren't just trendy marketing terms; they tap into deep psychological triggers that have influenced consumer behavior for ages. The idea of a limited opportunity can create a powerful attraction to a product, pushing people to act quickly for fear of missing out. In this chapter, we will dive into the history of these concepts and see how they've evolved into sophisticated strategies in today's branding world.

Using scarcity in marketing isn't a new concept; it has been a crucial part of sales tactics since commerce began. Long ago, merchants figured out that suggesting a product was in short supply could spark urgency among buyers. Picture a bustling village market from centuries past, where a vendor might call out, "Only three loaves of bread left!" The limited availability of bread would send the townspeople rushing to grab their share, worried that if they didn't act fast, they might go without. This simple story highlights a key psychological truth: the harder something is to get, the more appealing it becomes.

As transportation improved and markets grew, the ways to create a sense of scarcity became even more clever and impactful. With the rise of advertising in the late 19th and early 20th centuries, brands learned to craft perceptions of scarcity on a much larger scale. Take Coca-Cola, for instance, which cleverly created the illusion of scarcity through its limited-time holiday promotions, making certain drinks available only during festive periods. This strategy wasn't simply about selling soda; it was about building an experience that consumers looked forward to every year, deepening their loyalty through the allure of scarcity.

Fast forward to today, and we see how brands use scarcity with incredible precision. A perfect example is the streetwear brand Supreme, which has built its reputation on the concept of scarcity. By releasing a limited number of items each season, Supreme artificially creates a shortage that enhances the desirability of its products. Their famous "drop" model releases new collections just once a week, leading to long lines outside stores and a frenzy online. The psychological effect is significant: the fear of missing out on a unique item drives consumers to act fast and decisively.

Apple is another great example of using scarcity effectively. Every year, the tech giant launches new products that are not only highly anticipated but also available in limited quantities. When the iPhone is released, there's always a buzz in the air. Lines extend around the block as eager customers wait for their chance to grab the latest model, motivated by the belief that supplies might run out quickly. Apple has mastered the art of creating urgency through marketing, paired with the perception of scarcity, to build a loyal fan base that eagerly awaits each new release.

To truly grasp the psychological gears turning behind these behaviors, let's explore the scarcity principle. This key idea in social psychology states that people tend to assign more value to things they see as scarce. Research consistently shows that when consumers face limited choices, they often feel an increased desire for those options. A classic study by Cialdini and his team found that participants rated cookies in a jar as more desirable when there were only two cookies compared to when there were ten. This isn't just about cookies; it applies to all sorts of products, from luxury items to everyday goods and even experiences.

Urgency works alongside scarcity to drive consumer decisions. When shoppers believe they need to act quickly, the pressure to make a choice rises, frequently leading to impulse buys. Retailers have cleverly used tactics like countdown timers on websites, phrases such as "only a few left!" or "sale ends soon!" By fostering a sense of urgency, brands push consumers toward immediate decisions, often bypassing careful thought.

The emotional tug of scarcity and urgency becomes even stronger when we consider something called FOMO—fear of missing out. This feeling is especially heightened in our interconnected digital world, where social media constantly shows us what others are buying, experiencing, and enjoying. When someone sees friends flaunting a limited-edition sneaker or sharing moments from an exclusive event, the urge to grab similar experiences grows. This mix of social comparison and fear of exclusion makes scarcity and urgency even more effective in the branding landscape.

As we dig deeper into these strategies, it's also important to think about the ethical side of things. While using scarcity and urgency can effectively boost sales and build brand loyalty, it can also tip into an exploitative space. Consumers might feel rushed into making snap decisions, leading to buyer's remorse or financial strain. Striking the right balance between using these psychological triggers and practicing ethical marketing is a careful dance that brands need to navigate.

In the next part of this chapter, we'll look at how scarcity and urgency play out in various industries, recognizing both successes and cautionary tales. By examining real-world examples, we hope to help readers identify these tactics in action, leading to more informed choices as consumers. We'll also discuss how individuals can equip themselves with awareness, ensuring they make choices that align with their values instead of just giving in to marketing pressures.

Through this exploration, we aim to shed light on the complexities that come with the interplay of branding, consumer psychology, and ethical considerations. We want to give readers a richer understanding of the forces that shape their purchasing decisions. As we move into the next part of our discussion, remember to consider the historical roots, psychological principles, and ethical issues tied to the use of scarcity and urgency in branding. By looking at these different angles, we can truly grasp the power and influence of these strategies on consumer behavior. As we dive into the ethical questions surrounding urgency and scarcity strategies in marketing, it's clear these tactics tread a thin line between persuasion and manipulation. We need to think carefully about what these strategies mean—not just for businesses, but for consumers who often find themselves caught up in cleverly designed marketing campaigns.

A key question that comes up is whether brands are truly responding to what consumers want or if they are intentionally steering their behavior. This leads us to a deeper idea: the importance of making our own choices. Many people believe they're making informed decisions based on their wants and needs, yet the tactics used by brands can heavily influence those decisions. For example, imagine a countdown timer on a website, indicating a sale will end in just a few hours. This creates a rush, often pushing consumers to act quickly, driven by the fear of missing out, rather than taking the time to think things through.

This raises an important ethical question: when does creating urgency become deceptive? While urgency can indeed motivate action, it can also lead consumers to make hasty choices they might reconsider if given a moment longer. Brands must find a careful balance between generating excitement for a product and being transparent in their marketing messages. If a brand falsely claims there's limited stock just to create urgency, consumers may feel cheated when they find out the truth, leading to long-lasting trust issues.

Additionally, as brands tap into the emotions of their customers, the ethical concerns become even more complex. Are brands responsible for the anxiety, excitement, or regret their marketing stirs up? On one hand, brands might argue they are simply using psychological strategies to enhance the shopping experience. On the other hand, we must consider the possible harm when these strategies are misused. The emotional fallout from impulsive purchases—whether prompted by a time-limited offer or an inflated sense of scarcity—can leave consumers feeling regretful or financially stretched.

However, it's also vital to look at the more positive aspects of urgency and scarcity in the shopping experience. While these tactics can be seen as manipulative, they can also spark excitement and increased consumer engagement. For example, limited-time offers can motivate shoppers to act in ways they may have previously hesitated. Many consumers have successfully navigated the fast-paced world of sales and promotions, enjoying the thrill of a good find.

Take, for instance, the story of a young woman who stumbled upon an exclusive limited-edition sneaker drop scheduled to launch in just a few hours. The buzz around this release was electric, with collectors and fans chatting about it all over social media. For her, the sense of community surrounding the product only heightened her anticipation. She set reminders, connected with fellow sneaker enthusiasts, and within moments of the launch, she managed to snag the pair she wanted. This experience was not only rewarding but also deepened her loyalty to the brand. What started as a marketing push turned into a genuine connection with others who shared her passion.

While experiences like these highlight the potential upsides of urgency and scarcity, they also remind us that results can vary greatly. For some, the excitement of the chase brings joy as they acquire items that enhance their lives or reflect their identity. Yet for others, the pressure created by urgency can lead to snap decisions that result in buyer's remorse or financial difficulties. The difference in outcomes is striking, illustrating how the same strategy can provoke very different emotional reactions depending on the individual's mindset and situation.

As we prepare to discuss practical strategies for consumers to navigate the marketplace more thoughtfully, it's crucial to highlight the need for awareness when engaging with marketing that uses urgency and scarcity. Given the abundance of promotional messages, consumers need to develop the skill to recognize these tactics and understand what they mean. By becoming more aware, individuals can better evaluate their own decision-making processes and remain in tune with their wants and needs.

One simple tool to encourage this awareness is to take a pause before making a purchase, especially when faced with a time-limited offer. This moment of reflection can help shoppers determine whether they genuinely need or want the item or if they're simply reacting to the urgency created by the brand. Additionally, it's worth asking if the product will truly add value to their lives or if it's merely a passing desire fueled by fear of missing out.

Another helpful strategy is to do thorough research on products before making a buying decision. In today's world, where information is readily available, taking the time to compare options, read reviews, and evaluate pricing can lead to more informed choices. This approach not only empowers consumers with knowledge but also boosts their confidence in distinguishing genuine value from marketing tricks designed to spur impulse buying.

Discussing potential purchases with friends or family can also serve as a helpful sounding board. Sharing thoughts and concerns can clarify choices and help individuals avoid rash decisions driven by urgency. Encouraging consumers to question their motivations highlights how a thoughtful approach can lead to better purchasing decisions and a more rewarding shopping experience.

Ultimately, this chapter aims to give readers a clear understanding of how urgency and scarcity play a role in branding strategies. By merging psychological insights with ethical considerations, we can promote a more discerning mindset among consumers. Recognizing manipulative tactics while also appreciating the potential positives equips individuals to interact with the marketplace more mindfully and intentionally.

As we wrap up this exploration, it's evident that untangling the complexities of urgency and scarcity in marketing is anything but simple. While these strategies can lead to negative consequences, they can also enhance the consumer experience in meaningful ways. The key is to cultivate a nuanced understanding of these tactics, enabling us to make smart choices amid the whirlwind of consumerism. This empowers us not just to be passive buyers but active participants in our own shopping journeys, seeking out real value and forming deeper connections with the brands we choose to support. This chapter invites readers to reflect on their own experiences and consider how they can navigate the ever-changing world of consumerism with confidence and awareness. By unpacking the intricacies of branding and marketing strategies, we can nurture a more thoughtful consumer mindset that champions ethical practices and encourages meaningful interactions in the marketplace.

CHAPTER 7: HUMOR AND AUTHENTICITY

Throughout history, humor has played a vital role in how we communicate. From the earliest stories told around campfires to the slick ads we see today, humor has changed and adapted with shifts in culture, society, and technology. In a world where brands are fighting for our attention more than ever, using humor strategically has become an effective way for them to stand out, connect with us, and build lasting relationships. When done right, humor goes beyond just making us laugh; it can create real connections and a sense of authenticity between brands and their customers.

The way humor has evolved in advertising mirrors larger trends in society. In the early 1900s, ads were often straightforward and focused more on facts than feelings. As consumer culture began to grow, advertisers realized they could do more than just sell products—they could also touch hearts through humor. Over time, humor became an essential tool for brands, helping them break through the noise and forge memorable identities.

A notable milestone in the use of humor in advertising was Old Spice's "The Man Your Man Could Smell Like," which launched in 2010. This campaign was a game-changer for Old Spice, a brand that had long struggled with an outdated image. The ad featured the charming Isaiah Mustafa delivering a series of hilariously absurd monologues while seamlessly transitioning between wild scenarios. Thanks to its clever writing, surprising twists, and impeccable timing, the campaign revitalized Old Spice, demonstrating how humor could attract attention and change how people viewed the brand. It became clear that consumers were looking for brands that not only entertained them but also connected with their everyday experiences in a relatable way.

When we think about the psychological aspects of humor in branding, we can refer to established concepts like the Incongruity Theory. This theory suggests that humor happens when there's a gap between what we expect and what actually happens. In advertising, this often shows up through unexpected punchlines, ridiculous scenarios, or clever wordplay—all of which can make us laugh and stir up positive feelings. When we engage with funny content, we're more likely to associate those good vibes with the brand, which boosts our memory of them and makes us more favorable towards them.

To see just how effective humor can be, we can look at stories from consumers who remember their experiences with funny ads. For many, those humorous ads stick out in their minds, often outshining the more serious or straightforward ones. When we laugh, it creates a bond, making us feel more comfortable with the brand. In contrast to traditional ads, which can come across as skeptical or defensive, humorous content can disarm viewers, allowing brands to share their messages in a way that feels genuine and relatable.

However, brands need to be careful when using humor. The landscape of consumer perception is complex, and what one group finds funny may not resonate with another. This brings us to the idea of authenticity in branding. In recent years, authenticity has become increasingly important, with consumers valuing honesty and real connections over superficial marketing tricks. Nowadays, we're bombarded with ads, and we've become adept at spotting messages that feel forced or manipulative.

For brands to be seen as authentic, they need to understand that humor isn't a one-size-fits-all approach. It needs to be thoughtful, aligning with the brand's values and resonating with the target audience. A brand can craft a witty narrative, but if that humor doesn't reflect its core identity or comes across as insincere, it risks losing consumer trust. This shows how crucial it is for brands to find the right balance between engaging humor and genuine representation.

Dove's "Real Beauty" campaign provides a great example of blending humor with authenticity. Dove has consistently challenged traditional beauty standards, promoting a message that celebrates real women of all shapes, sizes, and backgrounds. While the campaign focuses mainly on authenticity, it also uses light-hearted humor to make the message more engaging and relatable. By weaving humor into its narrative, Dove encourages consumers to participate in discussions about beauty, leading to personal reflections that resonate deeply.

Transparency plays a key role in this conversation. In an age where we're more informed and connected than ever, brands that openly share their values and practices are more likely to build meaningful relationships with consumers. When brands are clear about their processes, ingredients, and intentions, it enhances the authenticity of their humorous content. This openness fosters trust, making consumers feel like they are part of a larger conversation rather than passive recipients of marketing messages.

When humor aligns well with authenticity, it can forge deep emotional connections with consumers. Yet, brands need to be cautious in their approach. The line between genuine humor and manipulative marketing can blur, and consumers can quickly spot insincerity. If a humorous ad feels forced or artificial, it may backfire, leading to negative views of the brand.

As we navigate this complex landscape, it's important for consumers to cultivate a sense of critical thinking when it comes to humorous advertisements. Just as brands need to be aware of their messaging, we should evaluate the content we see. Does the humor fit with the brand's values? Is it truly reflective of the experiences of its audience? These questions are crucial for understanding the role of humor in branding.

In the next section, we'll dive deeper into case studies that showcase successful blends of humor and authenticity in branding. We'll analyze the strategies behind these successes, which have led to greater brand loyalty and consumer engagement. Additionally, we'll look at the ethical dimensions of using humor in advertising, discussing potential pitfalls and urging brands to adopt practices that prioritize both engagement and integrity. Through these discussions, we aim to empower consumers with the knowledge they need to navigate the humorous world of modern advertising with a discerning eye. Humor is a powerful tool in branding, but it requires careful handling to avoid crossing the line into manipulation. As we dig into this subject, it becomes clear that while humor can create a sense of authenticity and friendliness, it can also backfire if it strays too far from a brand's true values. This is where we need to think critically about the ethical implications of using humor in marketing.

A key example comes from the controversial Pepsi advertisement featuring Kendall Jenner. This ad quickly became a textbook case of ineffective humor and a failure to align with genuine brand values. The commercial tried to take a light-hearted approach during serious social justice movements, but instead of resonating with people, it was criticized for being tone-deaf and exploitative. The backlash was immediate, showing that when a brand tries to use humor without a real connection to its principles, it risks creating a disconnect that consumers will notice right away. Pepsi's attempt to convey empathy and social responsibility through humor fell flat, serving as a warning for other brands that might consider similar tactics.

The contrast between humor and authenticity encourages us to think about the ethical duties of brands in their messaging.

Marketers need to realize that humor should not just be a clever trick; it should be an extension of the brand's identity, values, and dedication to its audience. To dig deeper into this, insights from marketing experts who specialize in consumer psychology are incredibly helpful. Their knowledge can guide brands on how to create humor that feels real and avoids the traps that can lead to negative consumer reactions.

Through interviews with these professionals, we'll uncover practical strategies for brands. One important approach is to ensure that any humorous content aligns closely with the brand's mission and values. When humor is genuinely connected to what the brand stands for, it helps build trust with consumers. They are more likely to respond positively to humor that feels authentic. Another important strategy is conducting thorough audience research that accounts for the cultural context and sensitivities of the target demographic. What makes one group laugh might not work for another, so brands need to be careful.

It's also crucial for brands to stay attentive and responsive to feedback when they use humor in their campaigns. Listening to consumer reactions—both good and bad—can provide insights that help refine their humorous messaging. This attentiveness not only boosts authenticity but also signals to consumers that the brand values their opinions and is committed to positive engagement.

In addition to these ethical considerations, the rise of social media has changed how humor is woven into branding strategies. Platforms like TikTok, Instagram, and Twitter have opened the door for content creation, allowing brands to interact with consumers more directly and in real-time. This shift has led to a new wave of humor-driven marketing campaigns that often invite audience participation, further enhancing the feeling of authenticity.

For example, Wendy's has built a strong online community by using humor in witty and often self-deprecating ways on social media. Their playful exchanges with followers show how humor can create a sense of connection and loyalty. The fast-food chain's success in this area demonstrates the potential for brands to build deeper relationships with consumers when humor aligns with a genuine voice. These interactions not only entertain but also make the brand feel more relatable, creating engagement that goes beyond simple transactions.

As we continue to navigate the changing landscape of humor in branding, it's important to recognize the risks of overdoing it. While humor is a great tool for engagement, brands need to avoid relying too heavily on gimmicks that could dilute their message or alienate their audience. Striking the right balance between being entertaining and staying true to the brand's message requires careful thought and planning. This is where the importance of strategic alignment with brand values comes into play.

In summarizing the main points we've covered so far, we see the critical need for maintaining a strong connection between humor and authenticity in branding strategies. As consumers are bombarded with humorous advertisements, they must develop a discerning eye that encourages thoughtful reflection. Questions about a brand's authenticity and how its humorous content aligns with its stated values can help consumers navigate the marketing world more effectively.

Looking ahead, it's clear that humor will remain a key player in branding. However, brands must adapt to new trends, including the growth of meme culture and the rising expectation for brands to engage authentically with social issues. Consumers are becoming more savvy, demanding transparency and accountability from the brands they choose to support. Humor can be a powerful way to address social issues, but brands need to approach these topics with care and a genuine commitment.

The message for brands is straightforward: focus on real engagement rather than superficial humor. The most effective branding strategies will be those that resonate authentically with consumers, building loyalty and trust. Brands that can skillfully navigate the complexities of humor while staying true to their values will likely shine in an ever-crowded marketplace.

In this deep dive into humor and authenticity in branding, we hope to enhance the reader's understanding of the delicate balance that must be maintained. By encouraging consumers to critically assess the humorous content they encounter, we aim to inspire a more thoughtful approach to branding. The mix of humor and authenticity is not just a marketing tactic; it reflects a brand's commitment to its audience and the values it upholds. As the marketing world continues to change, the brands that thrive will be the ones that engage authentically with their consumers through humor that truly resonates and fosters meaningful connections.

CHAPTER 8: THE POWER OF EMOTIONAL BRANDING

Every single day, countless shoppers stroll through grocery store aisles, browse online marketplaces, or navigate the busy streets of their cities, each driven by their own unique desires and needs. Among these individuals, something truly special happens: they form deep emotional connections with certain brands that go well beyond the basic function of a product. Imagine a parent wandering through a toy store, their gaze drawn to a bright package featuring a familiar logo. Suddenly, a wave of nostalgia hits them, bringing back memories of childhood playdates and birthday parties. Just seeing that brand sends them spiraling through a mix of emotions, linking cherished memories with current shopping choices. This phenomenon is the heart of emotional branding—a concept that extends beyond traditional marketing by building relationships that resonate on a profoundly personal level.

At its core, emotional branding is about crafting experiences that touch both the heart and mind of consumers. It goes way past the simple transaction of buying and selling, venturing into the realm of feelings, identities, and communities. When brands create a sense of belonging, they integrate themselves into people's lives in meaningful and lasting ways. This chapter will explore the different aspects of emotional branding, shedding light on its history, techniques, and the psychology behind why it's such an influential marketing strategy.

To truly grasp the concept of emotional branding, we first need to understand what it really means. Emotional branding refers to the practice of linking a brand to its consumers on a personal level, allowing emotions to influence their purchasing decisions. It's based on the understanding that emotions have a significant impact on human behavior and can be harnessed to build loyalty and attachment. Instead of merely promoting products, emotional branding invites consumers into a story, a community, and a lifestyle. It acknowledges that shoppers aren't just looking for things to buy; they are in search of experiences that resonate with who they are and what they aspire to be.

Branding has a long history that began with practical needs. In ancient times, craftsmen marked their goods with symbols to indicate where they came from or their quality. As societies developed, so did the idea of branding. The 20th century ushered in the age of advertising, where brands began to create identities, personalities, and narratives that went beyond just the products they sold. With the rise of digital marketing in the late 20th and early 21st centuries, this landscape underwent yet another transformation. Brands now have the means to tell their stories in a variety of ways, reaching consumers through social media, interactive content, and immersive experiences.

This evolution in branding has set the stage for emotional branding to shine. In today's competitive market, where many products are similar in quality and price, emotional connections can give brands a real edge. By telling captivating stories and creating experiences that resonate with their audience, brands can inspire loyalty that goes beyond price or product features. The ability to evoke feelings of joy, nostalgia, or inspiration can make all the difference when a consumer is deciding between one brand and another.

As we dive deeper into emotional branding, we should look closely at the techniques brands use to spark these emotional responses. One of the most powerful tools in this area is storytelling. A good story can break down barriers and connect with people. When consumers encounter a narrative that feels relatable, inspiring, or even touching, they are more likely to engage with the brand behind it. Consider Nike, a brand that embodies athletic excellence and resilience. Their marketing campaigns often showcase moving stories of athletes triumphing over challenges, pushing their limits, and achieving greatness. These tales not only highlight product features but also resonate with those consumers who strive to embody the same qualities in their own lives. By tying its brand to personal stories of success, Nike effectively taps into feelings of motivation and inspiration, building a devoted customer base that connects deeply with the brand's mission.

Another key technique in emotional branding is sensory marketing, which engages multiple senses to enhance the consumer experience and evoke particular emotional responses. Our senses—sight, sound, smell, taste, and touch—greatly shape how we perceive and interact with brands. For instance, think about the comforting aroma of freshly brewed coffee filling a café. This sensory experience not only brings feelings of warmth but can also entice customers to enter the store, making them more likely to linger and buy something. Retail environments are increasingly utilizing sensory elements to stir up desired emotions. A luxury skincare brand might use soothing scents and soft lighting to create a calm atmosphere, inviting consumers to relax and enjoy the experience.

Visual elements, like logos, colors, and overall design, also play a significant role in emotional branding. These visuals do more than just decorate; they act as symbols that convey deeper meanings and spark feelings. Take, for example, the iconic golden arches of McDonald's. Instantly recognizable, this symbol represents much more than fast food; it stands for convenience, comfort, and familiarity. Many consumers associate McDonald's with family outings, childhood memories, and joyful moments spent with loved ones. This emotional connection is reinforced by the brand's consistent messaging and imagery, which emphasize its identity as a place where memories are made.

  The relationship between emotions and consumer behavior is intricate, and it's crucial to understand the psychological factors at play. Emotions drive decision-making powerfully and often lead to choices that aren't entirely rational. When consumers associate positive feelings with a brand, they are more likely to develop loyalty and make repeated purchases. This is why brands that successfully establish emotional bonds can cultivate a devoted following that chooses them over competitors, even when there are other options available.

  To further understand these dynamics, we need to consider the idea of emotional memory. The emotional links we create with brands become ingrained in our memories, shaping our future actions. This is particularly true in moments of nostalgia when consumers tend to gravitate toward brands that remind them of cherished past experiences. For instance, many adults have fond recollections tied to a specific brand of cereal they enjoyed as kids. When they spot that brand on the grocery shelf, it can trigger a wave of positive emotions, leading them to buy it not just for the taste but for the memories it brings back.

As we transition into the next part of this chapter, it's crucial to recognize that emotional branding is not just an art; it's also a science. Brands that grasp the psychological principles behind emotional branding are better prepared to create messages and campaigns that resonate with their target audiences. For example, social proof is a powerful phenomenon that can enhance emotional connections. When consumers see others expressing happiness or satisfaction with a brand, it can spark similar feelings within themselves, creating a sense of community and belonging. This is often seen in the success of social media campaigns, where real consumers share their interactions with a brand, reinforcing its emotional appeal.

The techniques we've discussed so far are just the beginning. As we move ahead, we will explore additional strategies brands use to stir emotions and build lasting connections with consumers. From community-building to purpose-driven branding, there are many pathways through which emotional branding can come to life. It's a dynamic and ever-evolving field that reflects the complexities of human emotions and the changing marketplace. By delving into these techniques further, we will uncover how brands can create authentic connections that resonate deeply with consumers, ultimately influencing their choices and actions in the marketplace.

Exploring the depths of emotional branding reveals the subtleties of human psychology and the power of storytelling. As brands continue to refine their strategies, understanding how to forge emotional connections will remain essential for nurturing consumer loyalty and achieving sustainable growth. In the upcoming sections, we will continue to analyze the techniques of emotional branding, uncovering how brands can unlock the full potential of emotional engagement to build lasting relationships with their consumers.

The Impact of Emotional Branding on Consumer Loyalty

Emotional branding has become a vital approach in the competitive world of consumer marketing. Research shows that emotional connections established through branding can significantly boost consumer loyalty. Many studies reveal a strong link between emotional engagement and loyalty to a brand. For example, a report by the Harvard Business Review highlights that consumers who feel emotionally connected to a brand are more than twice as valuable as those who are just highly satisfied. Not only do these emotionally connected customers tend to buy more often, but they also become passionate advocates for the brand, influencing others through word-of-mouth recommendations.

To make this concept clearer, let's look at a few examples of brands that have truly excelled at emotional branding. One standout example is Nike, the iconic sports apparel brand. Nike's marketing campaigns have consistently inspired feelings of empowerment and motivation. Their famous "Just Do It" slogan resonates deeply with consumers, pushing them to challenge themselves and conquer obstacles. This emotional draw not only boosts sales but also builds a tight-knit community among athletes and fitness lovers. Nike has a remarkable ability to craft a story that aligns with personal dreams and ambitions, which has resulted in incredible loyalty, with customers forming a strong bond with the brand.

Another powerful case of emotional branding comes from Procter & Gamble (P&G), a global leader in household products. P&G's campaigns, particularly the touching "Thank You, Mom" series during the Olympics, tap into the deep emotions surrounding motherhood and family support. These ads showcase the love and sacrifices of mothers, forging a powerful emotional link with consumers. Because of this connection, shoppers are likely to choose P&G products not only for their quality but also because they resonate with the values highlighted in the brand's messaging.

In fact, a study from the University of Michigan found that brands that evoke strong emotional responses can boost customer loyalty by as much as 60%. This is especially relevant today, as consumers are faced with endless choices. Emotional branding helps cut through the clutter, leaving a lasting impression that encourages repeat purchases. Take Apple, for example. The brand has effectively created an emotional bond with its customers by promoting its products as essential parts of a lifestyle, not just tools. Their focus on creativity, innovation, and self-expression resonates on a personal level, making customers more likely to stay loyal to Apple for years.

Emotional branding doesn't just inspire loyalty and repeat purchases; it can also lead to brand advocacy, a powerful way to attract new customers. When people feel a strong emotional connection with a brand, they're more likely to share their positive experiences. This kind of organic promotion can greatly benefit a brand's growth. Nielsen reports that 92% of consumers trust recommendations from friends and family more than any form of advertising. Brands that successfully build emotional ties can leverage this trust to create a loyal customer base that actively promotes the brand to their friends and family.

However, while the positive effects of emotional branding on consumer loyalty are clear, it's also important to think about the ethical side of this powerful marketing tool. As we examine the ethical considerations around emotional branding, we need to recognize the potential for manipulation. Brands often have access to vast amounts of data about consumer behaviors and preferences, which can lead to tactics that exploit consumer vulnerabilities.

One troubling aspect of emotional branding is the potential for creating false narratives. Brands might paint an overly perfect picture to trigger emotional reactions, leading consumers to feel a connection that doesn't truly reflect the brand's values or practices. This disconnect can result in disappointment when consumers realize the truth about the brand's image versus its actual behavior. For example, a brand that claims to be eco-friendly but engages in environmentally harmful practices can leave consumers feeling betrayed when the truth comes out. This type of emotional manipulation is not only unethical but can also damage consumer trust and loyalty in the long term.

Moreover, emotional manipulation can occur when brands exploit vulnerable groups. For instance, marketing strategies aimed at individuals experiencing grief, loneliness, or financial difficulties can take advantage of these emotions for profit. While brands may claim to empathize with these challenges, the real intent might be to boost sales rather than to genuinely support consumers. This approach raises serious questions about the ethical responsibilities of brands and how they should handle their messaging in a way that is both true to their values and respectful of their audience's feelings.

The line between connection and exploitation can be quite thin. Brands that heavily rely on emotional storytelling risk crossing into exploitation if their messages don't align with their actual practices. A classic example of this disconnect occurs when companies position themselves as leaders in social justice, only to fall short in their internal practices or corporate social responsibility efforts. Consumers today are more aware than ever of these inconsistencies, and any breach of trust can lead to significant backlash. Social media amplifies this effect, allowing upset consumers to share their experiences, which can lead to rapid damage to a brand's reputation if it fails to uphold its stated values.

While it's essential to critique emotional branding, we should also recognize that not all emotional branding strategies are harmful. There are brands that genuinely strive to connect with their customers on an emotional level while maintaining ethical integrity. These brands prioritize honesty and authenticity in their communications, allowing consumers to build trust based on shared values. For instance, companies that support local communities, promote sustainable practices, and engage in charitable efforts show a commitment to their customers' well-being, which enhances the emotional connection in a sincere way.

As we wrap up our discussion on emotional branding, it's crucial to reflect on its dual nature. On one hand, emotional branding can create loyalty, advocacy, and community among consumers, deepening their engagement with brands. On the other hand, there's a real potential for manipulation and exploitation that requires careful scrutiny from consumers. Both brands and consumers have a role to play in navigating this landscape with care.

Consumers should take a moment to think critically about their emotional ties to brands. It's important to ask questions about the authenticity of the values a brand claims to uphold. Are these values truly reflected in their actions? How do they interact with their communities and the environment? By adopting a discerning mindset, consumers can empower themselves to make informed choices that align with their beliefs and values.

In closing, emotional branding is a powerful tool that can significantly influence consumer behavior. While it can create meaningful connections and foster loyalty, it also brings up important ethical issues. Brands that want to succeed in today's marketplace must focus on building genuine emotional connections while being transparent and accountable in their practices. This approach not only benefits brands in terms of customer loyalty and advocacy but also helps cultivate a marketplace that values integrity and authenticity. As consumers, we must stay alert, recognizing the impact of emotional branding while advocating for ethical practices that honor our feelings and choices.

CHAPTER 9: THE ETHICAL LANDSCAPE OF BRANDING

In today's consumer-driven world, branding goes beyond just logos, catchy slogans, or eye-catching ads. It has developed into a powerful force that shapes how we see products, influences our buying choices, and impacts our lives in significant ways. A perfect example of this is the story of Johnson & Johnson, a beloved brand that found itself at the center of a scandal that shook consumer trust to its core.

Back in 1982, Johnson & Johnson faced a crisis that would challenge its ethical principles and commitment to customers. After several tragic incidents involving Tylenol capsules laced with cyanide in the Chicago area, the company was thrust into a public relations nightmare. Instead of dodging responsibility or downplaying the situation, Johnson & Johnson took an unprecedented step by recalling 31 million bottles of Tylenol. This bold move would cost them about $100 million, but it showcased their dedication to transparency and their guiding principle known as "Our Credo." This principle emphasizes their responsibility to customers, employees, communities, and shareholders, marking a pivotal moment in corporate ethics.

This incident serves as a powerful entry point for our discussion on branding and ethics. It highlights how a brand's actions can either strengthen or undermine consumer trust. Ethical branding, as we will explore in this chapter, is about more than just following the law; it's about being open, honest, and respectful toward consumers.

As we journey through this topic, we will break down what ethical branding really means. At its heart, it is based on the moral values that guide a brand's actions and marketing methods. Ethical branding goes beyond just avoiding lies; it's about building trust and loyalty. Today's consumers are more informed and aware of their choices than ever before. Because of this, ethical branding is essential for forming real connections with customers.

Understanding ethical branding boils down to three key principles: transparency, authenticity, and responsibility. Transparency means that brands need to be open about their products, practices, and policies. Authenticity involves being real in messaging and actions, making sure brands don't mislead their consumers. Responsibility relates to the duties brands have toward society, which includes not only consumers but also the communities where they operate and the environment they impact.

In our fast-paced digital age, where news spreads rapidly and consumers have immense power through social media, the fallout from unethical branding can be swift and severe. For instance, many companies have faced backlash for engaging in greenwashing—the misleading tactic of promoting products as environmentally friendly when they are not. Brands that misrepresent their sustainability efforts often encounter public outrage, which can seriously damage their reputation and erode consumer trust.

As we dive deeper into the ethical implications of branding, we will introduce a framework called the "BS Intensity Spectrum." This spectrum categorizes branding practices based on their ethical consequences, ranging from "Creative and Honest" to "Deceptive and Manipulative." Each category represents a different approach to branding, varying in how transparent and honest they are.

On one end of the spectrum, we find brands that embrace creative storytelling and authentic messaging. These brands connect with consumers by creating narratives that reflect genuine values and commitments. They choose honesty over exaggeration, fostering relationships based on shared beliefs and real experiences. A great example is Patagonia, an outdoor clothing company known for its strong commitment to environmental activism. Patagonia doesn't just sell jackets; it actively advocates for the planet, encouraging consumers to think critically about their buying choices. This type of branding builds a genuine connection between the company and its customers, nurturing loyalty and trust.

On the other hand, we have the "Deceptive and Manipulative" end of the spectrum. This includes practices designed to trick consumers, often relying on fear-based marketing, misleading claims, or exploitative tactics. Some fast-food chains have drawn criticism for promoting unhealthy meals in ways that target children, effectively enticing young consumers to crave products loaded with sugar, salt, and unhealthy fats. Such strategies not only jeopardize the health of consumers but can also provoke strong backlash from parents and health advocates.

Knowing where a brand stands on this spectrum is crucial for consumers who want to make informed choices. It gives them the ability to critically assess branding messages and unravel the intentions behind them. It also serves as a wake-up call for brands, prompting them to reflect on their practices—are they making a positive impact on society, or are they purely focused on profit?

As we move ahead, we'll look at case studies that highlight both ethical and unethical branding practices, showcasing real-world examples that reveal the complexities of this landscape. These stories will provide insight into how brands can handle crises with integrity or, on the flip side, how they can falter by neglecting ethical considerations.

One inspiring case study features Ben & Jerry's, the ice cream company renowned for its dedication to social justice and sustainability. Throughout its history, Ben & Jerry's has boldly addressed various social issues—from climate change to racial justice. In 2020, following the tragic murder of George Floyd, the company issued a powerful statement about systemic racism and committed to donating proceeds to organizations fighting for racial equity. Their marketing not only promotes delicious ice cream; it represents a mission that resonates with an increasing number of consumers who value social responsibility.

In stark contrast, let's consider Volkswagen's emissions scandal. The car manufacturer was caught deliberately installing software in its diesel engines to cheat emissions tests, misleading consumers and regulatory bodies alike. The repercussions were swift and severe, leading to billions of dollars in penalties, numerous lawsuits, and a harmed reputation that would take years—if not decades—to mend. This incident stands as a stark warning about the consequences of unethical branding practices; deceptive tactics can result in public outrage and a significant loss of consumer trust.

The implications of branding ethics reach far and wide, affecting not just how consumers see brands but also shaping societal norms and values. As brands become more aware of their impact, the need for ethical branding practices grows stronger. It pushes brands to rethink their priorities—focusing not only on how to sell more products but also on how to contribute positively to society and the environment.

The road toward ethical branding requires brands to engage in meaningful conversations with their consumers, truly understanding their needs and values. This journey demands a commitment to ongoing improvement and openness to feedback, which allows brands to adapt their practices in line with consumer expectations. As we explore this chapter, we'll uncover practical strategies for brands aiming to enhance their ethical practices, ensuring they stay relevant and trusted in a constantly changing marketplace.

By promoting a culture of ethics and responsibility in branding, companies can build lasting connections with consumers that go beyond simple transactions. Ultimately, this trust can become a brand's most valuable asset, helping them flourish in a competitive environment while making a positive impact on society. Investigating ethical branding isn't just an academic exercise; it's a crucial consideration for brands wanting to align their practices with the values of today's socially conscious consumers.

As we continue to explore the world of branding ethics, we will look at the many ways brands can innovate and adapt their practices to meet these ethical standards. Through thoughtful analysis and a focus on real-world examples, we will shed light on pathways toward more ethically responsible branding, guiding both brands and consumers toward a more sustainable and trustworthy marketplace. Examining branding practices reveals a fascinating mix of persuasion and manipulation, especially regarding how they can influence consumer behavior. At the core of this discussion is the realization that branding is not just a way to identify products; it has transformed into a powerful tool that can sway decisions without people even realizing it. As brands compete for attention in an ever-crowded market, they often use psychological tactics that take advantage of our human weaknesses. These strategies might include creating a sense of urgency or tapping into our emotions, both of which can greatly impact what we choose to buy.

One common tactic is known as social proof. This principle plays into our natural instinct to look to others for guidance when making choices. When consumers see that a product is popular or has received a lot of positive feedback, they may feel pressured to jump on the bandwagon. Advertisers often use testimonials, celebrity endorsements, and user-generated content to craft a story that suggests, "Everyone is doing it." While this can boost sales, it raises important questions about authenticity. Are consumers making choices based on what they truly want, or are they simply going along with the crowd that branding encourages?

Another technique brands frequently use to create urgency is the illusion of scarcity. When a product is marketed as being in limited supply, it can trigger fear of missing out (FOMO), pushing individuals to act quickly to grab the item before it's too late. This kind of psychological manipulation can lead people to make purchases they might not have considered otherwise, forcing them to weigh their desire for the product against the worry of potential regret. This practice brings about significant ethical concerns. At what point does a brand's effort to enhance its appeal cross the line into unethical manipulation? It's a delicate balance that deserves careful thought.

Emotional appeals also play a huge role in how brands connect with consumers. By tapping into feelings—whether it's joy, nostalgia, or even sadness—brands can forge deep connections that resonate with people. Advertisements that tell a captivating story or evoke strong emotions can build strong brand loyalty. However, this emotional manipulation invites questions about the authenticity of that connection. Are consumers truly attracted to a brand's values and products, or are they simply reacting to a carefully crafted emotional experience designed to provoke a specific response?

Insights from behavioral economics help explain these dynamics, showing that people often make decisions based on mental shortcuts rather than careful thought. Brands can exploit these shortcuts to increase their influence. Understanding these psychological tricks not only helps consumers recognize when they're being manipulated, but it also encourages brands to reflect on their ethical responsibilities. The line between persuasion and manipulation is crucial to navigate, emphasizing the importance of adopting ethical practices that respect the choices of consumers.

In recent years, the conversation about corporate social responsibility (CSR) has added a new layer to the branding landscape. More and more, consumers are looking for brands that align with their values, support social causes, and contribute positively to society. This shift offers brands an opportunity to move past traditional marketing tactics and embrace ethical branding as a way to build trust and loyalty among consumers.

Brands that align their missions with social values not only stand out in the marketplace but also foster a loyal consumer base that feels personally connected to the brand's purpose. For example, companies like Patagonia have successfully woven environmental responsibility into their brand identity, attracting eco-conscious consumers. By advocating for sustainability and ethical practices, Patagonia has cultivated a reputation that resonates deeply with its audience, reinforcing the idea that ethical branding can provide a competitive edge.

The rise of socially conscious brands highlights how ethical considerations are increasingly influencing consumer choices. These brands often use storytelling to share their missions, creating a sense of community and shared purpose. By showcasing their commitment to social responsibility, they don't just attract consumers; they also instill pride in their supporters, which strengthens brand loyalty. This evolution reflects a broader cultural shift toward valuing transparency and ethical practices, prompting brands to rethink their roles in society.

As we consider these dynamics, it becomes clear that consumers have real power in the marketplace. By developing an awareness of ethical considerations, they can make informed choices about the brands they support. Encouraging consumers to question branding tactics, seek transparency, and prioritize ethics empowers them to hold brands accountable for their actions.

This call for ethical awareness goes beyond individual consumer choices; it represents a collective push toward a more conscientious marketplace. This shift isn't just a nice idea; it's essential for creating an environment where brands are motivated to adopt ethical practices. The implications of ethical branding are significant, setting a new standard for corporate responsibility in the eyes of consumers.

A hopeful perspective arises when we consider the potential for a shift toward ethical branding. The demand for socially responsible brands is likely to keep growing as consumers increasingly call for accountability and transparency. This cultural evolution paves the way for a marketplace where ethical practices are rewarded, and brands that prioritize social values can flourish.

As we look ahead to the next chapter, we should recognize that understanding the ethical implications of branding is just the beginning. Consumers also need practical strategies to navigate the complicated world of branding and consumerism. The upcoming chapter will explore these strategies, offering tools to help recognize and respond to ethical dilemmas in branding. This reinforces the idea that being aware and engaged is key to making informed decisions in a constantly evolving marketplace.

Through this exploration, readers will be encouraged to adopt a critical perspective on branding practices, empowering them to interact thoughtfully with the brands they encounter. The journey toward ethical awareness and responsible consumerism starts with understanding the nuances of branding's influence, ultimately leading to a more mindful approach to navigating the marketplace.

CHAPTER 10: BRANDING IN DIFFERENT INDUSTRIES

Branding is more than just a marketing tool; it's an art that changes shape depending on the industry. It's essential for businesses to understand that there isn't a one-size-fits-all approach to branding. Instead, companies need to tailor their strategies to fit the specific needs and characteristics of their industry. Factors like what consumers expect, the rules they must follow, and the cultural contexts they operate in deeply influence how brands are viewed and how effectively they communicate their messages. In this chapter, we'll take a closer look at how branding works in different fields, starting with an industry that has immense importance—pharmaceuticals.

When we think about the pharmaceutical industry, we enter a world where the stakes are incredibly high and the impact on public health is profound. Here, branding is all about trust and credibility. Consumers aren't just buying a product; they're putting their health and well-being on the line based on what pharmaceutical brands promise. This creates a branding environment where transparency, reliability, and ethics are absolutely critical.

The COVID-19 pandemic is a prime example of the power of branding in the pharmaceutical sector. Companies like Pfizer and Moderna didn't just create groundbreaking vaccines; they also had to tackle public perception and skepticism head-on. Their branding during this crisis highlighted how important it is to communicate messages that resonate with people's values and concerns. For example, Pfizer focused heavily on safety, effectiveness, and scientific integrity, which were crucial in building trust with consumers who were justifiably wary of a new vaccine.

These companies launched educational campaigns aimed at making the science behind the vaccines understandable. They took complex medical terms and broke them down into simple language that everyone could grasp. They also engaged healthcare providers as trusted advocates, knowing that endorsements from doctors and nurses could help reassure the public. Additionally, sharing testimonials from vaccinated patients helped to humanize the experience, showcasing real stories that underscored the significance of vaccination and the positive experiences of individuals.

However, branding in the pharmaceutical industry isn't without its challenges. The drive for profit is always there, but so is the responsibility to prioritize public health over financial gain. This balancing act raises important questions about how brands can promote products that are not only effective but also safe and ethically produced. A tragic example of this is seen in the branding of opioid medications, where aggressive marketing strategies led to widespread misuse and addiction. This situation has sparked a much-needed discussion about ethics in pharmaceutical advertising.

When we look at branding in this industry, it's clear that the implications are much bigger than just gaining consumer loyalty; they affect society as a whole. Brands must navigate this landscape with care, ensuring they build and maintain trust. The choices they make resonate far beyond the marketplace, impacting individuals, communities, and healthcare systems. This calls for pharmaceutical brands to adopt a long-term view of their identities.

Now, let's shift our focus to the food and beverage industry, which is full of life and driven by emotional connections and the lifestyles people aspire to. For many consumers, food is more than just something to eat; it's intertwined with their personal identities, cultural traditions, and ethical beliefs. In this context, branding thrives on storytelling—how a product fits into a buyer's overall narrative, dreams, and values.

Take Coca-Cola, for example. This brand has truly mastered the art of emotional branding. Over decades of advertising, Coca-Cola has woven itself into the fabric of popular culture as a symbol of happiness and togetherness. The bright red and white logo, paired with visually stunning ads showcasing joyful moments, has positioned Coca-Cola products as more than just drinks. They're experiences tied to fond memories. This emotional connection means that consumers aren't just buying a beverage; they're investing in a lifestyle filled with positivity and shared moments.

On the other hand, Whole Foods takes a different approach to branding that centers on health, sustainability, and ethical sourcing. This brand has built a strong identity around the idea of responsibly sourced food and living an environmentally conscious lifestyle. Their branding strategy resonates with the growing consumer awareness about health and the ecological impacts of food choices. With attractive packaging and informative labels, Whole Foods effectively communicates quality and reinforces its commitment to sustainability. They've cultivated a community of health-conscious consumers who align with their mission, allowing them to charge premium prices because people believe in the value of their products.

As consumer preferences shift toward healthier options, brands in the food and beverage world are adapting to meet these new demands. The rise of plant-based diets and clean-label products has changed the way brands define themselves. Companies are putting more emphasis on transparency in how they source their ingredients, aiming to build trust through authenticity.

Social media has also dramatically changed how brands connect with consumers in the food sector. Platforms like Instagram have created a space where visual appeal is everything. Influencers have become powerful brand ambassadors, shaping how consumers view products by sharing content that reflects their lifestyles. A well-placed product in an influencer's post can lead to a significant boost in sales, as followers want to emulate the lives they see online. This trend has encouraged food and beverage brands to expand their focus beyond traditional advertising to include partnerships with influencers who resonate with their brand values.

The visual elements of branding—like logos, packaging designs, and color choices—are incredibly impactful in this industry. Research shows that consumers often judge product quality based solely on packaging. An eye-catching product can evoke feelings of desirability, and brands that harness this effectively can gain a major competitive edge.

As we explore branding in the food and beverage sector, it's clear that emotional connections and lifestyle aspirations are key to successful branding strategies. Brands must stay flexible, continually adjusting to shifting consumer preferences while staying true to their core messages. Connecting with consumers on an emotional level can foster lifelong loyalty, making branding a crucial aspect of success in this ever-evolving industry.

In essence, the branding landscape is as varied as the industries it encompasses. Each field comes with its own challenges and opportunities, and grasping these nuances is vital for effective branding. The pharmaceutical industry requires an unwavering commitment to trust and ethics, while the food and beverage sector thrives on emotional ties and lifestyle aspirations. As we continue our journey into the fascinating world of branding, we will uncover the diverse strategies brands use across various sectors, illuminating the intricate relationship between branding and consumer behavior. In the lively world of fashion, branding is much more than just a marketing tactic; it's a vital part of who we are and how we see ourselves in society. With the captivating charm of luxury brands like Gucci and Chanel, the fashion industry showcases the rich layers of branding that go far beyond mere consumer products. For many people, slipping on a designer piece is about more than the clothing itself; it signals membership in a certain social circle and tells a story that connects with their personal values and dreams.

Luxury brands have mastered the art of creating an atmosphere of exclusivity and history, weaving tales that elevate their products to a level of desirability that often feels out of reach for the everyday shopper. Take Gucci, for example. Under the innovative guidance of Alessandro Michele, the brand has breathed new life into its image over the last few years. By embracing nostalgia and bold, eclectic designs, Gucci has attracted a younger audience while still honoring its roots. The brand's savvy use of social media and influencer partnerships has helped build a community around its offerings, drawing in consumers eager to connect with something bigger than themselves. This feeling of belonging can be a strong motivator, driving people to invest in items that reflect a certain image they wish to project.

Chanel, on the other hand, leans heavily on its narrative of heritage and craftsmanship. The tale of Coco Chanel remains central to the brand's identity, portraying her as a trailblazer of modern femininity and style. Take Chanel No. 5, for instance; it's not just a perfume, but a cultural icon that symbolizes elegance, sophistication, and empowerment. When someone chooses to buy Chanel, they aren't just getting a product—they're engaging with a legacy that resonates with their aspirations and values. This blend of storytelling and branding shapes how people view luxury items, forging an emotional connection that influences their buying choices.

However, the fashion world isn't only about luxury brands. The emergence of fast fashion has introduced a striking contrast in branding strategies that deserves our attention. Brands like Zara and H&M have changed the shopping landscape by prioritizing speed and affordability over exclusivity. Fast fashion thrives on current trends, quickly producing clothing that allows shoppers to refresh their wardrobes without breaking the bank. Yet the branding message here is quite different. While luxury brands focus on their rich heritage, fast fashion brands promote a narrative of accessibility and immediacy. This model speaks to consumers who feel the pressure to stay fashionable but may be limited by their budgets.

Zara, for instance, has positioned itself as a frontrunner in the fast fashion arena by adopting a business model that responds rapidly to consumer desires. Their ability to design, manufacture, and distribute new styles in just weeks creates a retail experience that feels fresh and exciting. However, this speed also raises ethical concerns regarding sustainability and labor practices. Fast fashion's quick production cycles often come at a cost, with many brands facing backlash over their environmental impact and labor conditions. Yet, despite these ethical dilemmas, the pull of fast fashion remains strong, highlighting the intricate nature of consumer behavior as it relates to branding.

The branding approaches of luxury and fast fashion brands reveal an interesting divide within the fashion industry, where consumer motivations intertwine with broader societal values. Luxury brands are skilled at crafting aspirational narratives, while fast fashion brands cater to a craving for immediacy and accessibility. This dynamic between exclusivity and inclusivity poses important questions for shoppers as they navigate their choices.

When we look closer at the branding strategies across the fashion sector, it becomes clear that the target audience plays a crucial role in shaping these narratives. Luxury brands generally aim for affluent consumers willing to spend on quality and heritage, while fast fashion appeals to a wider audience that values trends and affordability. This difference in target demographics influences everything from product design to marketing strategies, creating a unique environment for branding in each segment.

Additionally, the competitive landscape adds another layer of complexity to these branding strategies. Luxury brands often compete with each other to maintain high prices and a sense of exclusivity, while fast fashion brands fight for market share in a rapidly changing landscape full of shifting trends. This competition sparks innovation, prompting brands to refine their messaging and products to capture consumer interest and loyalty.

The rise of digital technology has also dramatically altered branding practices within the fashion industry. In a time when data analytics and social media dominate, brands now have unprecedented access to insights about consumer behavior. Luxury brands are using digital platforms to connect with their audience, creating immersive experiences that blur the lines between online and offline shopping. The art of storytelling has evolved in this environment—brands share behind-the-scenes glimpses, collaborate with influencers, and build communities around their products. This transformation empowers consumers to not only engage with brands but also influence the narratives that surround them.

Fast fashion brands are equally enthusiastic about digital transformation; they use analytics to tap into trends and consumer preferences. By understanding purchasing patterns, these brands can quickly adapt to what people want, ensuring their offerings stay relevant in a fast-paced market. However, this focus on data raises questions about privacy and the ethics of targeted marketing, especially in a world where shoppers increasingly seek transparency and accountability.

As we reflect on the dynamics of branding in the fashion industry, it's essential to consider how these strategies impact consumers. The stories crafted by luxury and fast fashion brands shape not just what we buy but also how we view our identities and place in society. The appeal of luxury items often lies in the status they confer, while fast fashion offers a connection to the ever-changing world of trends.

For consumers, wading through these branding messages calls for a discerning eye. It's vital to look beyond surface-level aesthetics and marketing gimmicks to grasp the deeper narratives and values that underpin each brand's efforts. As shoppers become more conscious of the ethical implications behind their purchases, they gain the power to make informed choices that align with their personal beliefs.

This awareness fosters a more thoughtful marketplace—one where consumers challenge the norm and hold brands accountable. By nurturing a critical perspective on branding, individuals can navigate the complexities of the fashion industry with greater understanding, leading to more responsible consumption choices. The influence of branding, while significant, can be directed towards positive change when consumers use their awareness as a guide for informed decision-making.

As we continue this conversation about branding, it's important to remember that the lessons learned from the fashion industry reach far beyond clothing and accessories. The principles that guide branding strategies resonate across various fields, shedding light on the intricate dynamics of consumer behavior. By learning from the narratives in fashion, we equip ourselves with valuable insights to engage thoughtfully with brands and their messages, paving the way for a more mindful and engaged consumer landscape.

CHAPTER 11: CULTURAL INFLUENCES ON BRANDING

Branding is more than just a clash of logos and catchy phrases; it's a rich and complex interaction deeply rooted in culture. To really understand how culture influences branding, we need to look at what culture actually means. Culture isn't just a collection of traditions or practices; it's made up of the values, beliefs, symbols, and behaviors that shape a community's identity. These elements are essential to how consumers behave and how they view brands. As we explore this chapter, we'll dive into how brands connect with cultural contexts, adjust their strategies to resonate with different audiences, and build strong relationships with their customers.

Let's start with an example that highlights both the challenges and successes a global brand faces when entering diverse cultural markets. Take McDonald's, for instance—a giant in the fast-food world that has made its mark in various countries across the globe. When McDonald's ventured into international markets, it faced the tough task of adjusting its menu to reflect local tastes and cultural preferences, all while keeping its brand identity intact.

In India, where many people follow vegetarian diets and consider cows sacred, McDonald's made the smart decision to remove beef from its menu. Instead, the company created unique offerings like the McAloo Tikki, which is a potato-based burger that suits the local taste. They also rolled out a variety of vegetarian dishes that not only appealed to local customers but also showed respect for the dietary values of the Indian population. This thoughtful strategy allowed McDonald's to thrive in a market that might have turned its back on a standard global menu.

Furthermore, McDonald's marketing in India reflects local customs and traditions. Their promotional materials often highlight local festivals, customs, and languages, demonstrating a true understanding and appreciation of Indian culture. By being culturally aware, McDonald's has not only established a strong presence in India but has also developed a loyal customer base that feels a genuine connection to the brand.

This method can be summed up with the concept of "glocalization." This strategy merges global branding with local cultural adaptations. Brands that embrace glocalization understand the significance of local contexts while trying to maintain a consistent global identity. Coca-Cola is another great example of glocalization. This iconic soda brand has effectively localized its marketing strategies in various regions, tweaking its messaging and product offerings to match local traditions and cultural symbols.

For example, during Ramadan in Muslim-majority countries, Coca-Cola's campaigns emphasize community, sharing, and family gatherings, aligning the brand's core values with the significance of this holy month. By connecting with local customs, Coca-Cola creates an emotional bond with its audience, enhancing its brand presence in a heartfelt way.

Coca-Cola also highlights local figures in its campaigns, whether they are musicians, athletes, or cultural icons. This approach not only makes the brand more relatable but also shows its respect for local culture. By featuring familiar faces, Coca-Cola communicates its understanding and appreciation of its consumers' culture, further cementing its place within the community.

However, the road of glocalization isn't always smooth. When brands expand into new markets, they can run into cultural challenges that lead to serious missteps. A notable example involves American clothing brands struggling in Japan. Many of these brands initially took a one-size-fits-all approach, assuming their established Western styles would easily appeal to Japanese consumers. This assumption overlooked the unique fashion preferences and sensibilities in Japan.

For instance, American brands that focused on casual wear and oversized styles found themselves out of sync with Japanese shoppers, who typically prefer tailored, form-fitting outfits. This cultural mismatch not only hurt sales but also caused backlash from local communities who felt that the brands didn't respect their fashion culture. The disconnect between the brand's image and the expectations of the local market serves as a powerful reminder of how crucial cultural awareness is in branding.

Brands really need to invest time in thorough research and cultural analysis before entering new markets. Gaining insight into the cultural landscape—including its values, symbols, and consumer behaviors—can help brands dodge potential pitfalls that might damage their reputation and trust with consumers. This evaluation should not just be a box to check on a marketing plan; it should be a continuous practice of cultural mindfulness.

Cultural research goes beyond just consumer tastes; it also involves understanding historical contexts, social dynamics, and even political environments that can shape how consumers view brands. For example, brands that enter markets with historical grievances must proceed with caution, ensuring their messaging doesn't inadvertently stir up past traumas or sensitivities. This approach requires brands to be observant, respectful, and responsive to the intricate realities of the cultures they are engaging.

As we continue to explore the deep connections between culture and branding, we'll also look at how the branding landscape is constantly evolving in response to global events. Cultural movements, social justice initiatives, and consumer activism increasingly shape how brands communicate their values and align themselves with the beliefs of their audiences. The demand for brands to take a stand on social issues has grown, particularly among younger consumers who actively seek brands that reflect their personal values.

In this shifting environment, brands must find the right balance between authenticity and commercial interests. When brands choose to advocate for social causes, they need to do so genuinely, avoiding the trap of performative marketing, where actions are just for show. Authentic engagement means truly committing to the causes they support, as consumers are quick to notice when brands fail to follow through on their promises.

Cultural influences on branding are incredibly powerful. They shape the strategies brands adopt, the messages they share, and the emotional bonds they create with their audiences. As we dive into more case studies and examples in the latter part of this chapter, we will see how various brands have skillfully navigated cultural landscapes, highlighting both their successes and the challenges they faced. Through these stories, we'll gain a deeper understanding of the importance of being culturally aware, the art of glocalization, and the changing expectations of consumers in a fast-paced world.

By the time we finish this chapter, you'll have a solid grasp of how cultural influences affect branding strategies and consumer behavior. We'll explore how brands can successfully connect with diverse cultures while keeping their global identities intact, reinforcing the essential role that cultural awareness plays in branding. Through this journey, we'll uncover how deeply culture impacts branding, positioning it as a key element in the ongoing conversation between consumers and the brands they choose to support. When we dive into the world of brand identity, one key element stands out: the powerful influence of cultural stories on how brands create their images and connect with consumers. At the core of this relationship is how brands can embed themselves in the narratives that resonate with people. Brands have evolved beyond mere names or logos; they have become storytellers that reach out to customers on a more emotional level.

A great example of this is Nike's iconic "Just Do It" campaign. Launched in 1988, this slogan quickly became more than just a call to promote athletic skill; it transformed into a powerful message of perseverance and empowerment that many people aspire to, especially when facing personal challenges or societal hurdles. The campaign has showcased stories of athletes overcoming obstacles, connecting with a wide range of consumers— from elite athletes to everyday individuals striving for self-improvement. Nike has positioned itself not just as a sportswear brand but as a symbol of empowerment, linking athleticism to broader movements that champion personal agency and resilience.

This knack for creating narratives around identity is essential for brands today, especially in a global marketplace where consumers crave authenticity. Nowadays, consumers are not just passive receivers of advertising; they are seeking connections with brands that reflect their values and aspirations. Brands that genuinely align their messages with cultural stories can build stronger relationships with consumers, creating loyalty that goes beyond mere transactions. The stories brands tell and the values they represent become key to their identity and play a crucial role in shaping how consumers see them.

As we look at the role of social media in this cultural branding landscape, it's clear that its impact on brand-consumer engagement is huge. Social media platforms have become the new spaces for cultural conversations, allowing brands to interact with consumers in real-time. They can respond to trends and engage in discussions that influence cultural narratives. This immediacy not only boosts a brand's visibility but also helps them become part of the conversations that matter most to their audiences.

Take Dove's "Real Beauty" campaign, for example. This initiative struck a chord during a time when traditional beauty standards were being challenged, opening up discussions around body positivity and self-acceptance. By featuring real women of various body types and backgrounds, Dove connected with a cause that resonated deeply with its audience, driving remarkable engagement and loyalty. The campaign not only improved Dove's brand image but also positioned it as a leader in social change, highlighting how effectively brands can use cultural stories to enhance their relevance.

However, the speed at which social media can amplify messages means that brands need to be especially mindful of cultural sensitivities and the risks of backlash. One misstep can lead to a viral uproar, as seen in various cases where brands have been accused of cultural appropriation or insensitivity. Such errors can have serious consequences, affecting how consumers perceive a brand and damaging their trust. Therefore, brands must navigate this landscape with cultural awareness, making sure their marketing strategies resonate positively within the communities they aim to engage.

Looking at branding strategies around the world reveals the complex relationship between culture and consumer expectations. Understanding these differences is crucial for brands that want to grow their presence globally. For instance, in

Western cultures, branding often highlights individualism, promoting personal choice, self-expression, and uniqueness. Companies like Apple have thrived by positioning their products as symbols of individuality and innovation.

Conversely, Eastern cultures tend to emphasize collectivism, where brand loyalty is often tied to social harmony, community values, and family connections. Brands in these regions may focus on group identity, showcasing how their products enhance social bonds or reflect shared values. The success of Coca-Cola in Asia, which often features themes of togetherness and family in their ads, emphasizes the importance of tailoring brand messages to fit local cultural expectations.

Another important aspect for brands to consider is ethical branding, especially in today's multicultural world. As consumers become more aware and socially conscious, they hold brands accountable for their representations and practices. The debate over cultural appropriation versus appreciation has become a significant issue in branding, pushing brands to find the right balance between drawing inspiration from diverse cultures and exploiting them for profit.

Ethical branding means committing to truly understanding and respecting the cultures that influence a brand. It's vital for brands to engage in genuine conversations with the communities they represent, ensuring their portrayals are accurate, respectful, and empowering. For instance, companies like Ben & Jerry's have taken steps to address social justice issues, using their platform to advocate for causes that resonate with their consumers. This strategy not only strengthens their brand identity but also reinforces their dedication to ethical practices within cultural contexts.

As we reflect on the dynamic relationships between culture and branding, it's clear that cultural intelligence is essential for brands wanting to succeed in a global market. Brands must tune in to cultural nuances, understanding how their messages will be received across different demographics and areas. The role of cultural narratives in shaping brand identity is crucial; they provide the foundation for how brands can engage meaningfully with consumers.

For consumers, this chapter highlights the importance of being mindful about their interactions with brands. Understanding the cultural narratives that brands project is vital for making informed choices. Consumers need to be aware of how branding affects their lives, recognizing how these narratives shape perceptions and influence behaviors. By being more conscious of these elements, consumers can navigate the complexities of the marketplace, choosing brands that align with their values and positively contribute to cultural discussions.

Ultimately, the relationship between culture and branding is complex, with significant implications for both brands and consumers. As brands adapt to cultural changes, it's crucial for consumers to stay alert and informed, ensuring that their interaction with brands promotes authenticity and accountability. Through this understanding, readers can empower themselves to recognize the cultural influences that shape their choices, becoming active participants in the conversation surrounding branding and culture.

In this ever-evolving landscape, recognizing branding as a cultural phenomenon will continue to develop. As new cultural narratives arise and consumer expectations change, brands will need to adjust and respond thoughtfully. This ongoing conversation between brands and consumers, grounded in cultural awareness and sensitivity, will play a vital role in shaping the future of branding in our interconnected world.

CHAPTER 12: THE FUTURE OF BRANDING

Branding is on the verge of an incredible change that will reshape how businesses connect with consumers and how we experience brands ourselves. Picture a day in 2030 when brands aren't just companies trying to get your attention. Instead, they'll feel like digital companions, woven into every part of our daily lives. Imagine strolling down a street where digital billboards don't just sit there—they notice you and even sense what you might want. As you near a café, a screen lights up, showcasing your favorite drink, plus a new pastry suggestion based on what you've ordered before. This isn't some futuristic fantasy; it's the new reality that's emerging thanks to technology.

The rapid changes in technology encourage us to take a closer look at what's happening right now. Augmented reality (AR), virtual reality (VR), and the Internet of

Things (IoT) are leading the charge, ready to change how brands interact with their audience. AR brings immersive experiences that allow consumers to see products right in their own spaces, making it easier to engage and boosting the chances of a purchase. Imagine a person wanting to buy a new sofa who simply uses their smartphone to see how it fits into their living room. They can easily change colors and styles with just a few taps. This kind of interaction not only makes shopping more fun but also removes a lot of the uncertainty that often comes with big purchases.

VR takes this idea even further by offering fully immersive experiences that pull consumers into different worlds. For example, luxury brands are starting to host virtual fashion shows, allowing people from all around the world to join in real-time. They can experience the thrill of sitting in the front row without ever leaving their homes. This approach not only keeps current customers engaged but also attracts new ones who might not have thought about the brand before.

At the same time, the IoT creates a network of connected devices that continuously share information between brands and consumers. Picture a smart fridge that tracks what groceries you have, suggests recipes based on those items, and can even order what you're missing from your favorite store. This kind of seamless integration builds loyalty, as consumers enjoy tailored conveniences that fit their lifestyles, deepening their emotional connection to the brand.

As we navigate these technological wonders, we can't overlook the essential roles that artificial intelligence (AI) and data analytics will play in shaping branding strategies. AI has a massive potential to enhance our understanding of consumer preferences, allowing brands to look beyond simple demographic categories and get a deeper sense of what individuals want. With machine learning, brands can analyze consumer behaviors and predict trends with impressive accuracy. For instance, imagine a fashion company using AI to sift through social media to spot trending styles. This enables them to adjust their inventory on the fly and create personalized ads that truly resonate with each consumer—an approach that feels tailored just for them.

The importance of big data in this context is huge. Brands have access to vast amounts of consumer data, allowing them to craft super-targeted advertising campaigns that cut through the noise of conventional marketing. When a consumer opens an app and sees ads that match their interests perfectly, the chances of them making a purchase skyrocket. But with this power comes great responsibility. It's vital to consider the ethics of data collection. Many consumers are concerned about their privacy, so being transparent about how brands use their information is key to building trust. Brands need to communicate their data practices clearly and offer consumers choices about how their information is used. Building this trust is essential for successful branding in the future.

As technology pushes us forward, it's also changing how consumers behave. We're seeing a shift towards a more connected society, where consumers have a wealth of information at their fingertips, making them more empowered in their shopping decisions. The rise of conscious consumerism is another significant trend. People today are prioritizing ethical sourcing, sustainability, and brands that align with their values. They're not just looking for products; they want brands that share their beliefs and contribute positively to society.

This shift means brands need to rethink their traditional marketing approaches. They can no longer simply advertise based on features and price. They must embody values that resonate with their audience. This is where storytelling comes into play. Brands that can effectively share their mission and show their commitment to social responsibility are more likely to build strong connections with consumers. For example, think of a brand that uses recycled materials in its products and is open about its supply chain. This not only attracts consumers who care about ethics but also fosters loyalty as customers feel they're part of something bigger every time they make a purchase.

Some brands have already adapted to these evolving consumer expectations. Take an outdoor clothing company that actively supports environmental conservation and donates a portion of its profits to protect natural habitats. Their messaging aligns perfectly with the values of their target audience, creating enthusiastic support and a community of brand advocates. On the other hand, brands that can't keep up with these changes risk fading into obscurity as consumers increasingly turn to those that demonstrate authenticity and accountability.

Looking at the future of branding, it's clear the stakes are higher than ever. Brands must adjust to the changing preferences of a more discerning consumer base, using technology while remaining committed to ethical practices. The integration of AR, VR, IoT, AI, and big data presents exciting opportunities for engagement, but it's those brands that prioritize transparency, authenticity, and social responsibility that will thrive in this new era.

The emergence of new technologies will undoubtedly transform the branding landscape, changing how consumers interact with products and services. But remember, it's not just about technological advancement. The future of branding also rests on our shared values—a movement towards a society that values connection, integrity, and purpose. As consumers grow more informed and empowered, brands can't rely solely on traditional marketing methods. For brands to survive in this increasingly complex marketplace, they need to evolve alongside their consumers.

In this light, it's essential for brands to regularly evaluate their impact and adjust their strategies as needed. By fostering genuine connections with consumers and aligning their practices with what truly matters to their audience, brands can thrive commercially and contribute positively to the world around them. The future of branding isn't just about selling products; it's about shaping culture, inspiring change, and creating a lasting legacy that resonates with consumers long after the purchase.

As we look forward, it's clear that the journey of branding is just beginning. With every new technological development, we stand on the brink of exciting possibilities—possibilities that will redefine not only how brands connect with their consumers but also how consumers view their world. Ultimately, it's up to both brands and consumers to find their way in this new landscape, making sure that as we move ahead, we do so with purpose, integrity, and a shared vision for a brighter future. The conversation around personalization versus manipulation is one that resonates deeply with how we relate to brands today. With the rise of advanced technology and data analytics, companies can craft incredibly personalized marketing strategies. While this can lead to enjoyable experiences for consumers, it also brings up important questions about ethics and how far is too far. As customers, we often find ourselves torn: personalized experiences can feel rewarding and designed just for us, making our connection with a brand feel real. Yet, there's a fine line where this personalization can tip into manipulation.

To better understand this tricky balance between personalization and manipulation, we need to consider the psychological effects of both. Personalization can genuinely improve our experience by making interactions feel relevant and special. Take streaming services, for example: when they suggest shows based on what we've watched, it feels like they truly get our tastes, enhancing our connection to the service. This connection can build loyalty and encourage us to engage more often with the brand.

However, there's a growing concern among consumers that too much personalization can come off as intrusive. In a world flooded with targeted ads that seem to know us better than we know ourselves, we begin to wonder: where do we draw the line? When brands gather extensive data to create detailed profiles about us—tracking everything from our shopping habits to our online activities—it can feel unsettling. Instead of feeling like unique individuals, we start to feel like mere data points. What began as a personalized experience can quickly become an uncomfortable invasion of our privacy.

Reflecting on our personal experiences can shed light on what feels acceptable versus what feels excessive. Many of us can relate to the feeling of browsing for a product online, only to be followed by ads for that exact item on various platforms. At first, this seems convenient—a helpful reminder of something we were interested in. But if those ads persist long after our initial curiosity has faded, it can quickly become annoying, trapping us in a never-ending marketing cycle.

For brands, this poses a significant challenge. They need to strike the right balance between personalization and the risk of manipulation, all while considering the ethical implications involved. Transparency is critical. Brands should be upfront about the data they collect and how they use it. When consumers understand that their information is being used to enhance their experiences rather than manipulate them, they are more likely to embrace those personalized efforts.

Moreover, brands should prioritize consumer choice. This means giving customers the power to opt into personalized experiences instead of making them the automatic default. By offering options, brands can respect the varied preferences of their audience. Some people may love highly personalized interactions, while others might prefer a more general approach. Allowing customers to choose how they connect with a brand fosters a sense of control and helps to create a healthier relationship.

The ethical challenges surrounding branding are further complicated by the growing use of artificial intelligence and big data. As these technologies become more integral to marketing strategies, brands face tough questions about authenticity. How can they ensure their branding remains genuine when algorithms are making decisions? This issue is especially pressing given the potential for AI to take advantage of consumer vulnerabilities.

Relying heavily on algorithms can also lead to biased practices if not carefully monitored. For example, if a brand typically targets a certain demographic, the algorithms might only reinforce that trend, potentially alienating other consumer groups. Brands must be vigilant to ensure their AI-driven strategies don't unintentionally exclude people or, even worse, perpetuate stereotypes.

To navigate this ethical landscape, brands need a framework grounded in transparency, education, and genuine connection. Transparency involves not only being clear about data usage but also sharing the ethical principles that guide branding decisions. Brands should openly communicate their values and show the steps they take to protect consumer interests.

Education is also key. Brands have the opportunity to inform consumers about the implications of data sharing and how it affects their experiences. By creating a culture of informed consent, brands can build trust and empower consumers to make conscious decisions about their interactions.

Additionally, building genuine connections is essential for ethical branding. Rather than treating consumers as mere data points, brands should strive to understand them as individuals with unique needs and experiences. This requires an emotional investment in the relationship, allowing brands to resonate on a deeper level. When brands prioritize authentic engagement, consumers are more likely to respond with loyalty and support.

As we think about the future of branding, it's important to remember it's not just about technological advancements. Each new innovation is an opportunity to build a more ethical and socially conscious marketplace. Brands shouldn't just focus on profitability; they should recognize their potential to positively impact society.

By embracing ethical branding principles, companies can thrive in an environment filled with scrutiny and heightened consumer awareness. They should aim to create experiences that genuinely resonate with their audience, built on a foundation of trust and integrity. For example, brands that engage in corporate social responsibility and prioritize sustainability can attract consumers who share similar values, deepening the connection.

An optimistic view of the future of branding combines technological progress with a commitment to ethical principles and trust. As consumers become more informed and discerning, brands must adapt to meet their evolving expectations. This shift will not only help brands stay relevant in a fast-changing marketplace but also empower consumers to engage meaningfully with the brands they choose.

To support this vision, both consumers and brands need to take an active role in shaping the narrative around branding. Consumers should feel empowered to express their needs and concerns, influencing how brands operate. At the same time, brands must listen and adapt, ensuring their strategies align with the values and expectations of their audience.

In the end, this chapter invites us on a collective journey towards a future where branding acts as a force for good—one that promotes positive change in society. As we navigate the challenges of personalization and manipulation, it's vital to keep ethical considerations at the forefront of brand conversations. By prioritizing transparency, consumer education, and genuine connections, brands can build relationships founded on trust and respect.

Together, we can reshape the branding landscape into one that meets the needs of consumers while also benefiting the greater community. The potential of branding is immense; it's up to us to harness that potential in a way that fosters meaningful change. As we look to the future, we must stay watchful, ensuring our experiences with brands reflect our values and aspirations, ultimately creating a marketplace that thrives on ethics and authenticity.

CHAPTER 13: CASE STUDIES IN SUCCESSFUL BRANDING

In today's fast-changing marketplace, grasping the nuances of branding is crucial for consumers and businesses alike. Case studies play a key role in this journey, shining a light on how brands tackle challenges, connect with their audiences, and influence buying habits. These real-life stories go beyond simple examples; they reveal the vibrant relationship between branding strategies and the realities of the market. By diving into these narratives, we can uncover valuable insights into the emotional, psychological, and social factors that drive successful branding efforts.

At its core, branding is all about its ability to connect with consumers on several levels. A strong brand does more than sell a product; it creates an experience, forges a connection, and sometimes even sparks a movement. The case studies we'll explore in this chapter showcase how brands have skillfully blended the art and science of marketing to reshape their identities and, in turn, revolutionize their markets. Throughout these stories, themes of emotional connection, innovative storytelling, and strategic responses to cultural changes will emerge, highlighting how brands have adapted to shifting consumer expectations while staying true to their core values.

One standout example of successful branding is Nike's "Just Do It" campaign, which launched in 1988 during a time when American culture was ripe for change. The late 1980s was a turning point in the U.S., marked by a growing focus on fitness, health, and individual empowerment. As the fitness movement took off, Nike saw a chance to motivate a generation eager to adopt a more active lifestyle. The simplicity and strength of the slogan "Just Do It" went beyond sports, transforming into a rallying cry for anyone looking to overcome obstacles and push their limits.

Nike's campaign wasn't just about selling shoes; it captured the essence of resilience and determination. The slogan resonated deeply with consumers who craved authenticity and motivation. It encouraged individuals to take action, embrace their potential, and reject complacency. This emotional bond set Nike apart from its competitors, making the brand synonymous with empowerment.

As the campaign progressed, Nike's ability to adapt became one of its greatest assets. Over the years, the brand has aligned itself with contemporary values, including a commitment to diversity and inclusion. By showcasing athletes from various backgrounds, Nike has broadened its appeal while reinforcing its message of empowerment. The brand's skill in responding to cultural shifts and weaving relevant social narratives into its campaigns has firmly established its position as a leader in the industry.

The "Just Do It" campaign highlights the incredible power of storytelling in branding. Each advertisement and promotional piece shared a story that resonated personally with consumers, fostering a sense of community around shared dreams. By featuring not only professional athletes but also everyday individuals on their fitness journeys, Nike created a narrative that many could relate to. This inclusion allowed consumers to see themselves reflected in the brand's message, forging a deep emotional connection that went beyond simple transactions.

When we look at Apple's branding strategy, it's clear that the company has also mastered the art of storytelling and emotional engagement. Apple's product launches have become events of great anticipation, known for their careful planning and execution. From the introduction of the first Macintosh computer to the latest iPhone, each launch is designed to build excitement and anticipation among consumers. The atmosphere at these events feels almost like a show, turning the act of revealing a new product into a captivating experience that draws in audiences worldwide.

Central to Apple's branding success is its focus on design and user experience. The company has built an ecosystem that transcends individual products, offering a lifestyle enriched by seamless integration and intuitive technology. Apple products are not just devices; they become extensions of their users' identities. This perception has been cultivated through thoughtful marketing that highlights simplicity, elegance, and functionality. Each product launch tells a story, showcasing not only the technical features but also the emotional rewards of being part of the Apple family.

What truly sets Apple apart is its knack for evoking strong emotional responses from its customers. The brand has cultivated a dedicated following that eagerly anticipates each new release, driven by both excitement and a desire to belong to something greater. Apple's marketing campaigns focus on stories that resonate with consumer aspirations and values, whether emphasizing creativity, innovation, or connection. By positioning its products as tools for self-expression and creativity, Apple has successfully elevated its brand beyond mere functionality, creating a sense of belonging among its users.

Additionally, Apple has effectively used exclusivity to boost its brand appeal. The company has cultivated an image of premium quality, which justifies higher price points and fosters a perception of value and status among consumers. This exclusivity is palpable; for many enthusiasts, waiting in line for the latest iPhone has become a cherished tradition. Apple's branding strategy has created a sense of community and connection, with customers eager to share their experiences and advocate for the brand.

As we dive into more successful branding case studies in this chapter, it's vital to recognize the common threads that weave these stories together. Both Nike and Apple have shown that effective branding goes beyond standard marketing tactics; it's about understanding human emotions, cultural contexts, and the ability to build connections that resonate deeply with consumers. As we explore further examples, we'll reveal how brands navigate challenges, seize opportunities, and ultimately shape consumer behavior through thoughtful and impactful branding strategies. **Case Study 3: Coca-Cola's "Share a Coke" Campaign**

Coca-Cola has always been known for its creative marketing efforts that resonate deeply with consumers. One of its standout strategies is the "Share a Coke" campaign, which kicked off in 2011 in Australia and eventually spread around the globe. This campaign signified a major change in Coca-Cola's branding approach, shifting the focus from just selling a product to building a personal connection with its customers. By swapping out its famous logo for popular names, Coca-Cola encouraged consumers to engage with the brand in a more personal way. Drinking a Coke evolved into a moment of sharing and connection.

What makes the "Share a Coke" campaign so brilliant is its simplicity and recognition of a basic human need: the quest for personalization and connection. By replacing the Coca-Cola logo with everyday names, the brand tapped into something deeply psychological. Suddenly, people weren't just looking at a generic product; they saw a bottle made just for them or someone special to them. This small tweak had a huge impact. Consumers felt recognized, appreciated, and relevant to the brand's story. It wasn't just about quenching a thirst; it became about sharing experiences and creating memories.

The emotional impact of the campaign grew even more with its integration into social media. People weren't just enjoying their Coke; they were sharing photos of their custom bottles online, forming a digital community around the product. The hashtag #ShareACoke took off, inviting individuals to post pictures of their uniquely named bottles and extending the campaign's reach. This interaction became a two-way street, allowing Coca-Cola to engage in the conversations that consumers were having, which fostered a sense of belonging that crossed geographical lines. The campaign effectively turned regular consumers into brand advocates, with every social media post acting as a personal recommendation for Coca-Cola.

The campaign's success is evident not only in the sales figures but also in the emotional connections it created. Coca-Cola saw a notable increase in sales in places where the campaign was launched, showing that people weren't just buying a drink; they were investing in an experience. The campaign reignited nostalgic feelings associated with Coca-Cola while also appealing to younger audiences who might have felt disconnected from traditional advertising methods.

Additionally, the "Share a Coke" initiative highlighted the importance of community and connection in branding. By leveraging content created by consumers, Coca-Cola created a feedback loop that not only promoted the product but also showcased the brand's flexibility in responding to consumer preferences and social trends. This campaign was more than just clever marketing; it represented a broader shift in branding towards a consumer-centered approach. This shift serves as a lesson for other brands, demonstrating the power of personalization, community engagement, and social sharing in crafting a memorable brand story.

Case Study 4: Dove's Real Beauty Campaign

In a stark contrast to the typical images of beauty often found in advertising, Dove launched its Real Beauty campaign in 2004, aiming to redefine what beauty looks like and promote body positivity. This groundbreaking campaign wasn't just about marketing; it became a social movement that sought to challenge the narrow definitions of beauty pushed by the beauty industry. By showcasing real women of different shapes, sizes, and ethnicities in their ads, Dove positioned itself as a brand that genuinely cares about its customers and their self-esteem.

Dove's motivations for this campaign were deeply rooted in the need to address the harmful effects of societal beauty standards on women's self-image. Research by Dove revealed that only 2% of women felt beautiful. In response, the brand wanted to start a conversation about beauty that included everyone and empowered individuals, thereby creating a stronger emotional connection with its audience. The campaign resonated with women seeking validation and sparked discussions about the unrealistic expectations often portrayed in media.

Authenticity and inclusion were key to the success of Dove's Real Beauty campaign. By using unretouched images and real-life stories, Dove delivered a message of empowerment that broke away from traditional marketing norms. This authenticity built trust and loyalty among consumers who felt seen and recognized. Dove was not just selling a product; it was championing a larger cultural shift. Over the years, Dove has continued to develop this message, launching initiatives like the Dove

Self-Esteem Project to further encourage self-love and body positivity among women and girls.

The impact of the Real Beauty campaign on consumer behavior and brand loyalty is significant. Dove successfully aligned its branding efforts with a social cause, raising awareness about the importance of diversity and representation in the beauty world. This alignment not only enhanced Dove's brand image but also positioned it as a leader in social change. By connecting with consumers on a deeper emotional level, Dove cultivated brand loyalty that went beyond simple purchases. Customers felt that by choosing Dove, they were supporting a brand that shared their values and beliefs.

Moreover, the Real Beauty campaign highlights how crucial it is for brands to align their strategies with societal values. In a world increasingly focused on representation and inclusivity, brands that embrace these ideals can reap considerable rewards. Dove's approach showed that meaningful engagement with social issues can lead to deeper connections with consumers, ultimately boosting brand loyalty and sales.

Key Takeaways and Lessons Learned

The case studies of Coca-Cola's "Share a Coke" campaign and Dove's Real Beauty campaign reveal several important lessons for both brand strategy and consumer awareness. First and foremost, the power of emotional connection cannot be overstated. Both brands tapped into essential human desires—connection and self-acceptance—crafting stories that truly resonated with their audiences. In a crowded market, forming emotional ties can be what sets a brand apart from others.

Another vital lesson is the importance of being adaptable. In today's fast-moving environment, brands need the agility to respond to consumer preferences and social changes. Coca-Cola's shift toward personalization demonstrates how a brand can update its approach to engage with modern consumers effectively. Similarly, Dove's commitment to promoting real beauty shows that brands must be willing to challenge societal norms and embrace authenticity. Being open to change can help foster a stronger sense of loyalty and trust.

Aligning brand narratives with consumer values is another valuable takeaway. Both Coca-Cola and Dove illustrated how branding can go beyond just promoting products to become a platform for social connection and change. By tying their marketing to broader societal values, these brands positioned themselves as advocates rather than mere sellers. This alignment not only fosters loyalty but also encourages consumers to connect with the brand on a personal level.

For consumers, these case studies remind us to look closely at branding. Understanding the motivations behind branding strategies can empower individuals to make informed choices. Being aware of the emotional and social dynamics at play can lead to more meaningful interactions with brands, allowing consumers to support companies that reflect their values.

When we reflect on the powerful impact of effective branding, it's clear that branding is a potent tool capable of inspiring, connecting, and empowering consumers. As shown by the case studies of Coca-Cola and Dove, branding can either build genuine relationships or manipulate consumer behavior. The stories crafted by these brands reveal the incredible potential of branding to influence not just purchasing choices but also societal perceptions and norms.

As readers navigate their consumer experiences, it's vital to approach branding with both appreciation and critical thinking. The lessons learned from these campaigns offer valuable insights into how branding serves as a strategic force. By recognizing the emotional connections, adaptability, and alignment with societal values, consumers can engage with brands in a more meaningful way while reinforcing their preferences and choices.

Ultimately, understanding the complexities of branding prepares consumers to navigate the marketplace with greater awareness. Branding is not just about logos and slogans; it's about the stories we tell, the communities we build, and the values we hold dear. Through these case studies, we gain a deeper appreciation for the intricate relationship between branding and consumer behavior, fostering a better understanding of how effective branding can shape market dynamics and societal conversations.

CHAPTER 14: EMPOWERING THE CONSUMER

Imagine a lively city waking up at dawn, buzzing with the energy of daily life as the sun rises over tall buildings. Among the sea of people rushing to start their day is Alex, a young professional who represents the modern consumer. As they head to work, Alex encounters a flood of branding messages—billboards showcasing the newest smartphone, the familiar logo of a beloved coffee shop, and the mouth-watering aroma of warm pastries from a nearby bakery. Each of these stimuli captures Alex's attention, subtly guiding their choices and shaping their perceptions.

In this moment, Alex's journey mirrors that of countless others in today's marketplace, where branding has become an ever-present force that influences decisions in both obvious and hidden ways. From the coffee they grab on the way to work to the car they dream of owning, branding acts as a silent guide, steering consumers like Alex in specific directions. Yet, as Alex navigates this tangled web of marketing, they begin to realize that not everything is as straightforward as it seems. The choices made are often swayed by carefully crafted stories that brands create to connect with consumers on emotional, psychological, and even social levels.

This chapter sets out to untangle the complexities of branding and empower consumers like Alex, giving them the tools to navigate the often confusing world of marketing with greater awareness. It's crucial for consumers to recognize that while branding can enhance their lives by providing identity and community, it can also manipulate desires and shape perceptions in ways that might not align with their true needs or values.

The journey starts with understanding the importance of consumer awareness. Many people, just like Alex, tend to operate on autopilot, allowing branding to dictate their choices without really thinking about them. Research from the American Psychological Association reveals that a staggering 80% of purchasing decisions are made subconsciously. This figure highlights how many consumers are often unaware of the powerful marketing strategies influencing their decisions. Recognizing this reality is vital for becoming more mindful consumers, capable of critically assessing the branding messages that surround us daily.

To illustrate the impact of branding, think about how a well-crafted advertisement can tug at our emotions. Consider a popular beverage brand that presents a sunny beach scene filled with friends laughing and enjoying their drinks. This imagery sparks feelings of joy, friendship, and relaxation. The brand isn't just selling a drink; it's offering an experience, an emotion that consumers long to feel. This method, known as emotional branding, taps into our desires for connection and happiness. Understanding these tactics is the first step toward taking charge in a world filled with sophisticated marketing strategies.

Looking deeper, we can identify some common branding strategies that consumers should keep an eye on:

1. **Emotional Appeals**: Advertisements often target our emotions—whether it's joy, nostalgia, fear, or pride. Brands carefully craft their messages to resonate with our feelings, making it essential for consumers to recognize when they're being influenced by emotional triggers. A classic example is holiday advertising, where brands evoke feelings of nostalgia and family togetherness, creating an emotional bond that can drive sales.
2. **Scarcity Tactics**: The idea of scarcity plays a significant role in consumer behavior. Marketers frequently create a sense of urgency with limited-time offers or exclusive products. For example, when a new sneaker model is released for a short period, this tactic not only boosts demand but also stirs up a fear of missing out, leading consumers to make impulsive choices. By recognizing these strategies, consumers can take a moment to consider whether their desire is genuine or simply a reaction to scarcity.

3. **Celebrity Endorsements**: There's no denying the influence celebrities have on consumer choices. Brands often bring in well-known figures to promote their products, using their popularity to attract customers. However, it's important for consumers to ask themselves if they're choosing a product because it truly meets their needs or just because a favorite celebrity is behind it. Taking a closer look at this influence can help lead to more thoughtful purchasing decisions.

These insights into branding strategies are crucial for developing a more discerning consumer mindset. However, awareness alone isn't enough. To navigate the complexities of branding effectively, individuals must also build their critical thinking skills when it comes to making purchases.

The next section will focus on practical strategies that inspire critical reflection before buying something. Engaging in self-reflection can shine a light on personal motivations and outside influences, helping consumers better understand what drives their choices. Here are a few questions to ponder:

- **What needs does this product fulfill?** This question encourages consumers to evaluate whether a product truly meets a real need or desire, helping to differentiate between what's essential and what's impulsive.
- **How is this brand positioning itself in relation to my values?** By considering how a brand's values compare to their own, consumers can make more informed choices that align with their personal beliefs.
- **Am I being swayed by marketing tactics?** This question prompts consumers to think about whether their decision-making process is being influenced by emotional appeals or scarcity tactics, fostering a deeper awareness of outside pressures.

By weaving these reflective questions into their decision-making process, consumers can cultivate a proactive approach to branding. Instead of being passive recipients of marketing messages, they can engage critically with brands, ensuring that their choices genuinely reflect their values.

As Alex carries on with their day, they may find themselves at a crossroads. Standing before the coffee shop, they recall a recent marketing campaign showcasing the brand's commitment to sustainability. While they appreciate this message, they also remember their desire to support local businesses and make eco-friendly choices. Here, Alex's newfound awareness prompts them to reflect: "Does this brand really align with my values, or am I just attracted to its clever marketing?"

This inner dialogue highlights how the strategies discussed can become a vital part of the consumer experience. By questioning their motivations and the branding messages they encounter, consumers are empowered to make informed choices that truly reflect who they are, enhancing their engagement with the marketplace.

The journey of empowerment doesn't stop with self-reflection. It's equally important for consumers to share their insights and experiences with others. In a world increasingly shaped by branding, talks about consumer experiences can foster collective awareness and encourage others to adopt a critical approach to branding. Engaging in conversations with friends, family, or online communities can create a ripple effect, inspiring more people to recognize and navigate the complexities of branding.

As we look ahead, it's important to remember that branding isn't inherently bad. Instead, it serves as a tool that can enhance consumer experiences and build connections. By practicing critical thinking and awareness, consumers can navigate branding strategies with intention and purpose, making choices that resonate with their values and desires.

In the next section, we'll explore more actionable steps consumers can take to deepen their understanding of branding, empowering them to become informed participants in the marketplace. Practical exercises can be incredibly helpful for empowering consumers. They enable individuals not just to notice how branding affects their shopping choices, but also to actively engage with and understand these influences. One effective exercise is creating a personal brand diary. This diary serves as a reflective tool where people can jot down their purchases, whether it's everyday items like groceries or bigger buys like electronics. By tracking their spending alongside the branding messages that influenced their decisions, consumers can uncover valuable insights into their motivations.

For example, when someone buys a new pair of sneakers, they can note not just the brand name but also the feelings that swayed their choice. Was it an eye-catching ad they saw on social media? Did a celebrity's endorsement catch their attention? Or maybe the brand's commitment to sustainability aligned with their own values? This kind of reflective practice not only fosters awareness but can lead to significant changes in shopping habits over time, as people start to recognize which brands truly resonate with their beliefs and which ones don't.

Another practical step consumers can take is to research the brands they frequently buy from. This can start with a simple online search to learn about a brand's history, values, and practices. Are their products ethically sourced? What are their labor conditions? How do they address environmental concerns? By digging deeper into the stories behind their favorite brands, consumers can empower themselves with knowledge. Equipped with this information, they can make informed choices and possibly shift their buying habits toward companies that are committed to ethical practices.

Furthermore, the strength of community should not be underestimated. When individual actions combine, they can create a strong force for change. This section will highlight inspiring examples of consumer movements that have successfully challenged unethical branding practices, showing how people can unite to drive real change.

One notable example is the Fair Trade movement. What started as a grassroots initiative to ensure fair wages and better working conditions for farmers and artisans in developing countries has grown into a major influence in global consumerism. Through educational campaigns and dedicated advocacy, supporters have pushed brands to adopt fair trade practices, resulting in a more equitable marketplace. This illustrates how united consumers can encourage brands to rethink and often improve their practices.

Social media has played a key role in these movements. Platforms like Twitter and Instagram have become essential tools for advocacy, where consumers can shed light on unethical branding and rally support. Hashtags like #BuyLocal, #EthicalFashion, and #SustainableLiving have created communities of like-minded individuals committed to making a difference, inspiring others to reconsider their consumption patterns.

On a local level, initiatives like farmers' markets, which promote local produce and sustainable farming, or clothing swaps aimed at reducing waste, are great ways to foster community spirit and empower consumers to make choices that reflect their values. Participating in these movements encourages individuals to think critically about the brands they support and the impact of their purchases on the broader world.

As we look ahead at the future of consumerism, it's crucial to recognize the significant changes happening in the marketplace. The growing demand for ethical brands and sustainable practices signals a shift in consumer values. More and more people are realizing the importance of aligning their buying decisions with their ethical beliefs, giving rise to a trend known as conscious consumerism. This isn't just a passing fad; it reflects a larger societal movement toward prioritizing values over blind loyalty to brands.

Brands that emphasize sustainability, like Patagonia and TOMS, have gained popularity not only for their products but for their dedication to social and environmental responsibility. Patagonia's commitment to environmental activism and TOMS' "one for one" model, where they donate a pair of shoes for every pair sold, resonate with consumers who are increasingly seeking authenticity and purpose in the brands they choose. These companies illustrate how blending purpose with profit can forge powerful connections with customers.

As consumers become more aware and critical of traditional branding strategies, they naturally seek out brands that reflect their values. This transition to ethical consumerism marks a new chapter where businesses are held accountable not just for their products but also for their overall impact on society and the environment.

In this changing landscape, it's important for consumers to harness their purchasing power. Each decision to support an ethical brand adds to a larger movement, encouraging more businesses to adopt sustainable practices. This shift in consumer behavior empowers individuals, making them feel that their choices truly matter. They are not just passive recipients of branding messages but active participants in shaping the marketplace.

Reflecting on Alex's journey using these strategies creates a compelling story. By keeping a brand diary and conducting thorough research, Alex began to notice patterns in their shopping behavior. Initially swayed by catchy advertisements and social media influence, Alex gradually moved toward a more conscious approach to consumerism.

Over time, Alex became involved in community initiatives, attending local farmers' markets and advocating for ethical brands. This engagement not only expanded their understanding of branding but also deepened their commitment to supporting businesses that align with their values. The transformation was profound; Alex no longer felt like a victim of manipulative branding. Instead, they approached shopping with a critical eye and a proactive mindset, equipped with the tools to navigate market complexities.

CONCLUSION

As we conclude our journey through the intricate world of branding, let's return to that moment in the store, standing before the sleek, white box with the apple logo. Armed with the insights from this book, you now see beyond the surface. You recognize the psychological triggers at play, the visual cues designed to evoke specific emotions, and the social dynamics influencing your desire.

This newfound awareness doesn't diminish the power of branding, but it does change your relationship with it. You're no longer a passive recipient of brand messages, but an active, discerning participant in the marketplace.

Remember, brands can be forces for good, fostering innovation and positive change. But they can also exploit vulnerabilities and perpetuate harmful stereotypes. As informed consumers, we have the power to shape the future of branding through our choices and our voices.

So, the next time you encounter a brand message, pause. Reflect on what you've learned. And make your decision not just as a consumer, but as an empowered individual shaping the world around you. Your journey to becoming a more conscious consumer has only just begun.

www.ingramcontent.com/pod-product-compliance
Lightning Source LLC
Chambersburg PA
CBHW052150220526
45471CB00004B/1611